A SIMPLE FEAST

A SIMPLE FEAST

a YEAR *of*
STORIES & RECIPES
to SAVOR & SHARE

DIANA YEN &
The JEWELS *of* NEW YORK

ROOST BOOKS
Boston & London
2014

Roost Books
An imprint of Shambhala Publications, Inc.
Horticultural Hall
300 Massachusetts Avenue
Boston, Massachusetts 02115
roostbooks.com

9 8 7 6 5 4 3 2 1

First Edition
Printed in the United States of America

♾ This edition is printed on acid-free paper that meets the
American National Standards Institute z39.48 Standard.
♻ Shambhala Publications makes every effort to print on recycled paper.
For more information please visit www.shambhala.com.

Distributed in the United States by Random House, Inc.,
and in Canada by Random House of Canada Ltd

Designed by Lisel Arroyo

LIBRARY OF CONGRESS CATALOGING-IN-PUBLICATION DATA

Yen, Diana.
A simple feast: a year of stories and recipes to savor and share / Diana Yen.
pages   cm
Includes index.
ISBN 978-1-61180-032-6 (hardcover: alk. paper) 1. Cooking, American.
2. Cooking—New York (State)—New York City. 3. Seasonal cooking. I. Title.
TX715.Y33 2014
641.59747—dc23
2013021956

CONTENTS

BIOGRAPHY

⇥⇤

The Jewels of New York, founded in 2009, is a creative studio led by Diana Yen that combines a love of cooking with the beauty of everyday things. Diana's work is expressed through food styling, photography, menu consulting, and special event catering.

The studio aims to uncover the hidden treasures New York has to offer and share them with others through seasonally based cooking. Diana strives to bring the same sense of warmth found in good home cooking to her clients through catering and menu development services.

Diana's projects with leading lifestyle magazines and design-savvy clients focus on the simplicity and elegance of everyday meals. With a background in home and lifestyle design, she strives to bring a sense of beauty and community to the table.

PRELUDE

⤝⤞

IT BEGAN IN A BASKET

In the beginning, before we started The Jewels of New York, my friend Lisel Arroyo and I were just a couple of pals in Brooklyn with old Schwinns and bicycle baskets taking rides to our favorite destination: the farmers' market. In the springtime beet greens spilled over the edges of our totes, while radishes rubbed up next to just-picked strawberries and sugar snap peas so sweet we'd devour them before we made it home. In the summer curvy cucumbers and fat tomatoes filled our bellies. Autumn meant apples and orchard hopping. In wintertime we found warmth in our pantry with stewed beans and hearty pastas. Life in New York was a hustle, but on the other side of our welcome mat we found solace in a warm stovetop and a room of our closest friends to muffle the noise of the busy city outside. Much has changed since then, and at the same time not a stitch is different. Lisel has moved to Columbia and become my dearest pen pal as we continue to collaborate on design projects from afar. Over time, I've become a true food professional, and my grocery lists are much longer. My clients have become friends whom I look forward to working with week after week.

The Jewels of New York grew from a passion for sustenance in every sense of the word. With my creative background in fine art and design, I fed myself with the beautiful objects around me, the projects I poured myself into, and the artistic community I lived in. As a lover of food, I fed myself with the elaborate dinner parties I would throw with my artist friends. But I was still hungry.

Freshly arrived from laid-back California, New York and its energy filled my appetite for adventure. Every neighborhood held the possibility of a new discovery, and my curiosity sent me on a whirlwind journey around Manhattan and upstate New York, where I began to learn not only about different culinary traditions, but also about myself as a cook. I discovered that I love simple food that centers around the ingredients rather than solely the technique. I devoured my new home. Queens was my Chinese hot pot kingdom, Chinatown was my banh mi go-to, and Little Italy made my burrata dreams come true. New York pulled me in, and I have yet to escape its enchantment. With the foods that were filling my bicycle basket, I wanted to create a fantasy like the ones I experienced through my adventures. And so, with my passion for aesthetics and a desire for creative pleasure, The Jewels of New York, a studio that provides consultation and styling for food savvy clientele, was born. It's become a business that I run every day, but it's also an excuse to do what I love best—play with food.

The studio is where my team and I develop new recipes inspired by our finds at the farmers' market, the seasons, and the flux of New York City's energy. Our opinions differ and our tastes vary, but the excitement of creating new dishes and discovering new ingredients brings us together; that is what makes a day at work interesting. For us the act of cooking is comfort. A day with the Jewels means shopping for ingredients, tasting, making sense out of recipes and our imaginations, photographing our creations, and escaping into the fantasies that drove us from the start. When the day is done, the dishes washed, and the last crumbs brushed away, we nibble on the leftovers with our elbows on the counter and feel rewarded with having created something beautiful and delicious.

FROM A BASKET TO A BOOK

This book is a journey into my ideal New York year. In these pages you will find the produce that once filled my bicycle basket, but that has since been refined into dishes that are perfect for small gatherings, a treat for yourself, or an intimate dinner with someone special. I chose to format this book around the seasons because that is how I like to cook, enjoying each ingredient at its peak.

With this book, I offer up my passion for beautiful simple fare and that sense of togetherness that is celebrated in feasting with friends. Wherever you live, I encourage you to take inspiration from your surroundings and challenge and stretch your culinary intuition. As the seasons turn over, embrace the changing weather, eat foods when they are ripest, and give yourself up to the pleasure of dining with those you love.

AUTUMN

On the motionless branches of some trees, autumn berries

hung like clusters of coral beads, as in those fabled

orchards where the fruits were jewels.

CHARLES DICKENS

APPLE PICKING

⚞⚟

*T*here's no better time of year than autumn to take a day trip outside the city. The summer heat has loosened its grip, the anticipation of holidays musters excitement, and leaves pop with color. And apples are ripe for picking: McIntosh, Cameo, Golden Delicious, Macoun, Honeycrisp, Mutsu; green, red, and maroon speckled; squat, tall, fat, and full of juice. All are sweetest in autumn.

Each year around this time, my friends and I pack a blanket, a couple of sandwiches, and several homemade dipping sauces for apple tasting and settle into the car for a drive to an apple orchard to get in tune with our edibles. I like to visit Maskers Orchard, two hours north of Manhattan near Harriman State Park. Scattered among bales of hay, the sounds of farm animals mingle with the smell of apple cider. We follow the trail of fallen apples to the trees they once hung upon, and through the branches we climb to the top of the trees where the best apples wait. There's something special about reaching into the places no one else has gotten to.

When our baskets are full, we sit down for a picnic and slice into our harvest. No two apples taste the same. Cortlands make the sides of our tongues jump from their tartness. Pearl white–fleshed and incredibly sweet, the juice of Macouns runs down our arms and into the crevices of our elbows. Honeycrisps are apple perfection; sweet, crisp, and transcendent with a sprinkling of sea salt.

When the sky turns golden and the sun begins to descend, it's time to head home. With our sandwiches devoured and the jars of sweet dip wiped clean, we load bushels of apples into the trunk and pile back into the car, riding our apple high back to the big city. As we drive home from our upstate adventure, the rear bumper threatening to skim the roadside from the weight of our apple load, we bask in our hand-picked reward, one that is not only sweet but brings us closer to where our food comes from.

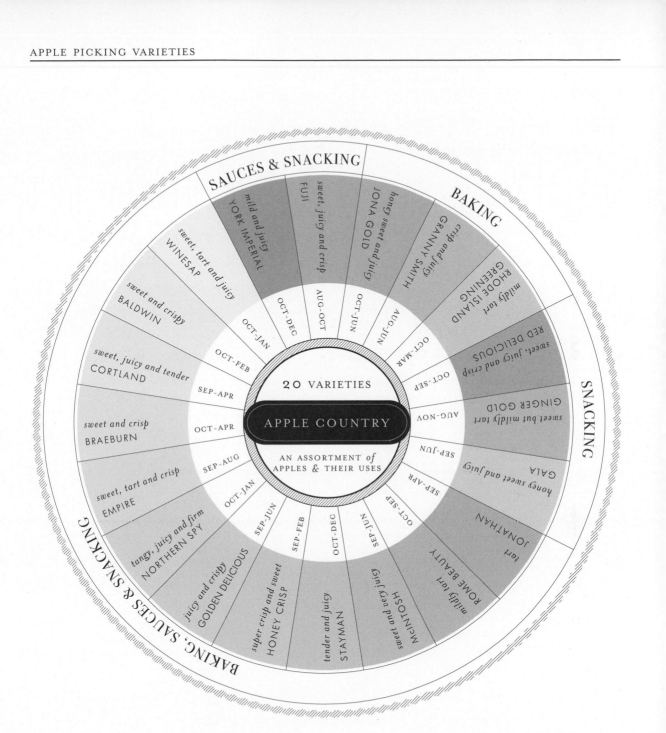

Chart No.001

Raw Kale Salad *with* Pecans *and* Golden Raisins

Serves 4

Kale is the king of leafy greens. This powerhouse veggie is packed with vitamins K and C, beta-carotene, and calcium. When kale becomes a farmers' market staple and the leaves are at their crispest and most nutritious, I enjoy it in its raw form, particularly when I can find Tuscan kale (also known as dinosaur or lacinato kale) or any type of baby kale.

To dress up this salad I've thrown in pecans for their rich, buttery quality, golden raisins for their understated sweetness, and a few Parmesan shavings to round out the mélange. It's a great salad to serve alongside any meal.

$^1/_3$ cup golden raisins

1 bunch baby kale or Tuscan kale, stalks removed and discarded

Finely grated zest and juice of 1 lemon

1 garlic clove, grated

½ cup extra virgin olive oil

Salt and freshly ground black pepper

2 tablespoons roughly chopped toasted pecans

Parmesan cheese shavings for topping

In a small bowl, soak the raisins in hot water to cover for 10 minutes to plump them, then drain completely.

Meanwhile, slice the kale into ¾-inch ribbons and place in a large bowl. In a small bowl, whisk together the lemon juice, lemon zest, garlic, and olive oil. Season with salt and pepper.

Scatter the pecans and golden raisins over the kale, add the dressing, and toss. Let sit at room temperature for 15 minutes—this allows the kale leaves to soften and absorb the flavors of the dressing. Top with Parmesan shavings and serve.

Sweet Potato *and*
Apple Dumpling Soup

Serves 4 to 6

Nothing is as soul warming as handmade dumplings served in a steaming hot bowl of soup. When the autumn breezes begin to chill, this soup is perfect fare for an early evening dinner on the patio with your favorite quilt around your shoulders and a couple of close friends to warm the air.

These tangy orange zest—laced dumplings are tossed in a little browned butter to add a rich nutty note, and they are finished with a scattering of fragrant crisp sage, perfect for including in any harvest feast.

Canola oil for frying

1 bunch fresh sage

Salt

1 medium sweet potato, peeled and cubed

1 Granny Smith or Golden Delicious apple, peeled, cored, and quartered

1 large egg, beaten

1 teaspoon brown sugar

¼ teaspoon freshly grated nutmeg

Finely grated zest of 1 orange

1 cup packed grated Parmesan cheese (about 4 ounces)

¾ cup all-purpose flour, plus more as needed

4 cups Basic Vegetable Stock (page 26) or Homemade Chicken Stock
    (page 93; or substitute a good-quality packaged broth)

1 ham hock (optional)

Ground white pepper

Wash and dry sage; pick the leaves off the bunch and set aside. Pour canola oil into a medium saucepan to a depth of ¾ inch and place over medium-high heat. When the oil begins to shimmer, lower the heat to medium and add the sage leaves, in several batches, and fry for 10 to 15 seconds each, until crisp. Transfer to a paper towel–lined plate, season with salt, and set aside until ready to use.

Place the sweet potato and apple in a large saucepan. Add water to cover and a large pinch of salt, place over high heat, and bring to a boil. Reduce the heat to medium-low and simmer for 15 to 20 minutes, until cooked through. Drain and transfer to a large bowl. Add the egg, brown sugar, ¼ teaspoon salt, the nutmeg, orange zest, and Parmesan and mash to combine the ingredients well. Gradually add the flour a spoonful at a time, stirring until the batter is stiff. On a floured surface, roll the dough into a ¼-inch-thick log. Cut the log into ½-inch pieces, and with your hands, form the logs into little dumplings. Place the dumplings on a wax paper–covered baking sheet, dust with flour, and set aside.

How to Make

BASIC VEGETABLE STOCK

Makes about 2 quarts

1 tablespoon olive oil; 2 onions, quartered; 5 celery stalks, cut into 2 inch pieces; 2 large carrots, peeled and cut into 2 inch pieces; 1 head of garlic, halved; 2 leeks, washed, trimmed, tough outer leaves removed; 3 sprigs fresh thyme; 3 sprigs flat leaf parsley; 1 bay leaf; 1 teaspoon whole black peppercorns.

HEAT THE OLIVE OIL IN A LARGE STOCKPOT over medium high heat. Add the vegetables and cook for 5–8 minutes, stirring occasionally, until the vegetables begin to brown. Add the herbs, bay leaf, and peppercorns and cover with 4 quarts of water.

Bring to a boil, reduce heat, and simmer, stirring occasionally for 1 hour or until the broth is reduced to about 8 cups. Remove from heat and strain stock through a fine sieve and discard solids. Once cooled, stock can be stored covered in the refrigerator for 4 days or frozen for up to 3 months.

Pour the stock into the pan, add the ham hock, if using, place over high heat, and bring to a boil. If you are using a ham hock, reduce the heat and simmer for 1 hour, then remove the ham hock. If you're not using the ham hock, just bring the stock to a boil, gently lower the dumplings into the broth using a slotted spoon, cover, and simmer for 3 minutes, or until the dumplings are cooked through and float to the surface. Ladle the soup into bowls, season with pepper, and garnish each bowl with a scattering of crisp sage.

Pork Chops *with* Sautéed Apples

Serves 4

The smell of pork chops flavored with toasted fennel sizzling on a stovetop always brings up cozy memories of family meals, me rushing to finish my homework in time for dinner as my mom clanked away in the kitchen. No matter how busy everyone was, Mom brought us together at the end of each day over our dinner plates.

Here the sweet, spiced apples balance out the savory flavor of the pork. Any variety of apple will work here; cooked slowly with butter and cinnamon, the apples will melt in your mouth and leave a trace of syrup on the plate that begs to be wiped up with a forkful of pork.

FOR PORK CHOPS

2 tablespoons fennel seeds

2 teaspoons salt

2 teaspoons freshly ground black pepper

Four ¾- to 1-inch-thick bone-in center-cut pork chops

2 tablespoons extra virgin olive oil

FOR THE SAUTÉED APPLES

2 tablespoons unsalted butter

2 medium apples, peeled, cored, and cut into ½-inch-thick slices

2 shallots, thinly sliced

¼ teaspoon ground cinnamon

½ cup apple cider

½ cup Madeira wine

Toast the fennel seeds in a large skillet over medium heat for 1 to 2 minutes, until fragrant. Transfer to a plate to cool, then grind the seeds in a mortar with a pestle. Stir in the salt and pepper to make a dry rub.

Pat the pork chops dry with a paper towel and coat the chops on both sides with the dry rub.

Heat the olive oil in a cast-iron skillet over medium-high heat. Add the pork chops and sear until they brown, about 3 minutes. Turn over and brown well on the second side, about 3 minutes. Transfer to a plate.

In the same skillet, melt the butter over medium heat. Add the apples, shallots, and cinnamon and sauté until the apples and shallots soften and caramelize, 5 to 7 minutes. Stir in the apple cider and Maidera and bring to a boil. Lower the heat, return the pork chops to the pan, and cook until the pork chops are tender, with an internal temperature of 145°F, about 10 to 15 minutes, turning them halfway through. Place the pork chops and apples on a plate, loosely cover with foil, and set aside. Keep cooking the juices in the pan until they are reduced a bit and shiny. Plate the pork shops with the apples, drizzle with the sauce, and serve.

Apples *with* Dipping Sauces

When I go apple picking, my favorite tradition is to pack along an assortment of dipping sauces. After climbing and snipping and harvesting my apple loot, I lay out a blanket, slice into the bounty, and have an apple tasting right there in the orchard. With the bright colors of the apples, the little wooden pairing knives, and the mason jars of sauces, it's as picture perfect a scene as it is delicious.

BOURBON CARAMEL SAUCE

I cup sugar

3 tablespoons water

4 tablespoons unsalted butter

½ cup heavy cream

2 tablespoons bourbon

In a medium saucepan, combine the sugar and water. Place over medium heat and cook until the mixture begins to boil and turns a deep amber color, about 6 minutes. Add the butter to the pan and stir until it melts into the syrup. Take the pan off the heat and slowly add the cream, stirring constantly, until smooth. Stir in the bourbon. Pour the sauce into a heatproof jar and cool to room temperature. To serve, dip fresh apple slices into the caramel and sprinkle with flaky salt (I like Maldon or fleur de sel). The sauce can be made ahead of time and stored in an airtight container in the refrigerator for up to I week.

CHOCOLATE HONEY SAUCE

½ cup heavy cream

6 ounces bittersweet chocolate, chopped

2 tablespoons honey

½ teaspoon vanilla extract

Pinch of salt

In a small saucepan, combine the heavy cream, chocolate, and honey. Place over low heat and stir constantly until chocolate is melted and the sauce is smooth. Stir in the vanilla and salt. Pour the sauce into a heatproof jar and cool to room temperature. To serve, dip fresh apple slices into the chocolate sauce. The sauce can be made ahead of time and stored in an airtight container in the refrigerator for up to 1 week.

BROWN BAG LUNCH

⟅⟆

The packed lunch is an art form that is crafted and perfected by parents everywhere, each bringing to it their own special touch. My parents moved here from Asia, so my packed lunches were always a toss-up between Chinese and American foods.

Sometimes I would reach into my backpack and find sticky jam spread all over my homework. Digging deeper, I would find my lunch bag trapped beneath textbooks. My mother would try her best to make me the perfect peanut butter and jelly sandwich, but by the time I got to it, it was usually smashed into a single layer of sweet gooeyness that I would eat it straight from its plastic wrapping in an effort to keep my fingers clean. The sandwich was often accompanied by a bag of potato chips or, on test days, a Fuji apple for luck. Other days my mom would pack leftovers from our family dinner from the night before. It could be anything from my favorite curry noodles to handmade dumplings, or congee with salty peanuts and a black egg that freaked my classmates out every time. Condensed milk with butter on toast and hot Ovaltine in a Thermos were afternoon snacks I grew to treasure. My lunch bag always held a surprise, and what made it really special was that the food inside was made and packed just for me by my mother.

As adults, we still deserve a little nod of comfort now and then. While Mom may not be doing the packing, there's no reason not to make something special for yourself. The recipes that follow are grown-up versions of the classic bag lunch—pack them up as a treat to comfort yourself on a long day away from home, or eat them at your table and reminisce over your favorite childhood lunch memories.

Homemade Ginger Ale

Serves 4 to 6

There are days when nothing but the fizz from a soda will do. As a tonic for upset stomachs and thirst, ginger ale does the trick every time. Homemade ginger honey syrup makes this sweet treat more wholesome than the canned variety. The ginger honey syrup is a great staple to have on hand in the fridge: Simply mixed into bubbly water or along with an added spirit of your choice, you have a refreshing drink ready to serve.

    ½ cup honey
    ½ cup water
    ½ cup peeled and chopped ginger
    4 to 6 lemon wedges
    Soda water
    Ice cubes
    Bitters

In a small saucepan, combine the honey, water, and ginger. Place over medium-high heat and bring to a rolling boil, then reduce the heat and simmer for 10 minutes. Remove from the heat and steep the ginger in the syrup until cooled completely, about 30 minutes. Strain the syrup into a storage container and discard the ginger. The ginger syrup can be made ahead of time and stored in an airtight container for up to 1 week.

To make ginger ale, squeeze the juice from a lemon wedge into each glass along with 2 tablespoons ginger honey syrup and top it off with soda water. Finish with a few ice cubes and a dash of bitters. To make this soda to go, funnel it into an empty glass bottle with a screw cap or pour it into a Thermos.

Roasted Turkey, Manchego,
and Fig *and* Onion Jam Sandwiches

Serves 4

Even as an adult, a homemade sandwich hits the spot like not much else—it's familiar and economical, and best of all it tastes like home. Fig and onion jam sets this sandwich off with a sweet and savory note, while Manchego adds an edge of nuttiness. Feel free to swap in another jam, such as apricot, if you don't have fig jam on hand. The jam recipe will provide you with more than enough for your sandwiches and makes a great accompaniment to other roasted meats and poultry for the rest of the week.

FOR THE FIG AND ONION JAM

2 tablespoons extra virgin olive oil

I medium sweet onion, thinly sliced

Pinch of salt

½ teaspoon red pepper flakes

¼ cup sugar

¼ cup apple cider vinegar

½ cup fig jam

I baguette

FOR THE SANDWICH

Dijon mustard

I cup mixed baby greens

12 ounces sliced roast turkey

2 ounces Manchego cheese, shaved

To make sweet onion jam, heat the olive oil in a medium saucepan over medium-low heat. Add the onion, salt, and red pepper flakes and cook, stirring occasionally, until the onion softens and becomes translucent, about 5 minutes. Stir in the sugar and vinegar, increase the heat to medium-high, and bring to a rolling boil. Reduce the heat and simmer until the liquid has evaporated and the onions are caramelized, about 10 minutes. Transfer to a small bowl and stir in the fig jam. Let cool. The jam can be made ahead of time and stored in the refrigerator for up to 5 days.

Cut the baguette into 4 pieces lengthwise and then cut each in half widthwise. Spread 4 bottom slices of bread with a smear of mustard, followed by some greens, turkey slices, and cheese shavings. Spread the jam over the remaining bread slices and assemble to make sandwiches. I like to wrap these sandwiches in parchment paper and fasten them with baker's twine; they travel well this way and look like pretty little parcels.

Root Vegetable Chips

Serves 4 to 6

These colorful chips make a playful addition to any brown bag lunch. Experiment with a variety of root vegetables such as fingerling potatoes, lotus roots, or sunchokes to find your favorites. Making your own chips requires some patience, but the result is well worth it. Note that the secret to the crispest chips is to pat your vegetables as dry as possible before frying.

> Peanut oil for frying
> 1½ pounds mixed potatoes, such as Yukon gold potatoes,
>   purple potatoes, and sweet potatoes
> 1 medium beet, peeled
> Flaky salt for finishing

Using a mandolin set to 1/8 inch, slice the vegetables into thin rounds. Place the vegetables in a colander and gently rinse them of excess starch, then thoroughly pat dry.

Pour peanut oil into a medium saucepan to about 3 inches deep. Heat the oil over medium-high heat to 325°F as measured by an instant-read thermometer, or until a drop of water sizzles in the pan. Add the vegetable slices in small batches without overcrowding the pan. Fry until light golden brown, 1 to 2 minutes. Using a slotted spoon, transfer the chips to a paper towel–lined plate. Season with salt and let cool.

The chips are best eaten the day they are made. Store any leftovers in an airtight container. I divide them up by the handful into wax paper bags to accompany sandwiches.

Espresso Chocolate Chip Cookies

Makes about 4 dozen cookies

These cookies, my version of the classic chocolate chip cookie, are one of my fa-vorite recipes of all time. I came up with the idea one day when I was in a cook-ie-baking mood and was digging around for chocolate in my pantry. I came across a bag of chocolate-covered espresso beans, and voila! I decided to add them to my cookie dough instead of chocolate chips. The crunch of the espresso bean adds texture to the cookie while still giving you a chocolaty bite. They're at their best when eaten straight out of the oven with the chocolate melted and a bit of flaky sea salt sprinkled on top, but they also make a perfect lunch bag treat.

    2 cups all-purpose flour
    ½ teaspoon baking soda
    ½ teaspoon salt
    ¾ cup (1½ sticks) unsalted butter, melted and cooled
    1 cup packed light brown sugar
    ¼ cup granulated sugar
    1 large egg
    1 large egg yolk
    1½ teaspoons vanilla extract
    ½ cup chocolate-covered espresso beans

Sift the flour, baking soda, and salt into a medium bowl.

In the bowl of an electric mixer, beat together the butter, brown sugar, and granulated sugar on medium speed until well combined, 1 to 2 minutes. In a sepa-rate bowl, beat the whole egg and egg yolk with the vanilla. Reduce the mixer speed to low and slowly add in the egg mixture. Beat for another couple of seconds or so, until well combined. Add the flour mixture, ½ cup at a time, then, using a wooden spoon, gently stir in chocolate-covered espresso beans.

Divide the dough in half and place each half onto a sheet of parchment paper. Shape the dough roughly into logs about 10 inches long. Fold the parchment over each log, and using the edge of a ruler, press and roll the dough to form a 1½-inch log. Seal with the parchment and chill in the freezer until firm, about 1 hour.

Preheat the oven to 350°F. Line 2 large baking sheets with parchment paper.

Unroll the cookie dough log from the parchment and cut the logs into ¼-inch-thick discs. Arrange the discs onto the baking sheets, spacing them about 2 inches apart. Bake, one sheet at a time, for 13 to 15 minutes until the edges of the cookies are browned. Transfer the cookies to a wire rack to cool completely. The cookies can be stored in an airtight container for up to 5 days.

Note: Chilling the dough firms up the butter, which makes it easier to work with later. Resting the dough will let the gluten "relax," helping to make cookies that are softer and less dense. The dough can be stored in the freezer for up to a month for freshly baked cookies anytime.

TREASURE HUNT

I love the thrill of hunting down the aisles of a flea market or vintage store—you never know what treasures you might uncover. Gently worn objects glow with the varnish and history of the many hands that have held them before, and listening to stories told by the market merchants fuels my fantasy of a world filled with objects from the past. Sometimes an object will speak to me and convince me to make it part of my collection. When I get it home, I polish it up and take pleasure in putting it to use.

I've always been inspired by the tools we use in nourishing ourselves. A steak knife that was made by an artisan has the ability to transform an everyday flank steak into artfully cut slices of tender meat. Cornichons never taste so good or look so perfect as when eaten off the tip of a nineteenth-century French spear made just for this purpose. The same can be said of a spoon made specifically to serve mustard, or a butter knife that's been used to slide through churned wares for centuries. Unlike kitchenware manufactured for the masses, these tools for eating have, like homemade foods, a distinct human touch.

One of my favorite ways to spend a Saturday is knee deep in the Antiques Garage in Chelsea, where I visit one of my favorite treasure collectors, Andre Burgos, a true curator of culinary instruments. In his booth there are jelly jars from Paris pantries circa the 1870s, a model of the *Normandie* built by his grandfather, a collection of copper mold rarities, and cutlery designed to meet every purpose. Andre enchants his customers with his endless knowledge of old objects and his passion for collecting, and I rarely walk away empty handed. His entire booth gleams decadently with polished silver, always leaving me entranced. At times I've gathered fish knives with beautiful etchings and pearl handles, carving sets perfect for a roast, and pocket knives that I keep handy in my back pocket on a shoot. No matter what I end up bringing home, I find a way to make it part of everyday life. I give it a polish and look forward to using it at my next meal, paying homage to its maker.

Duck Rillette

Makes about 4 cups

The process of transforming game into rillettes is ancient, and it has survived for a reason. (Rillettes are meat that is cubed or chopped, salted and cooked slowly in fat until very tender. They are then shredded and blended with cooking fat to form a rustic paste.) Take the time to explore this recipe and you'll understand why. Rillettes take on a deep bronze color after slow cooking for several hours, and when smeared over toast, the rich textured spread will melt away in your mouth. If duck isn't available, try using pork or chicken instead; the flavor will be different but still smooth, creamy, and divine.

TIME: *Overnight curing, 3½ hours cooking time*
SPECIAL EQUIPMENT: *Four 8-ounce canning jars, sterilized*

¼ cup coarse sea salt

¼ cup sugar

2 tablespoons chopped fresh thyme leaves

2 tablespoons chopped fresh rosemary leaves

Finely grated zest and juice of 1 orange

4 duck legs (about 3 pounds total)

2 medium shallots, sliced ¼ inch thick

2 garlic cloves, crushed with the side of a chef's knife and peeled

1½ cups dry white wine

3 to 4 cups homemade chicken stock or good-quality packaged broth

¾ cup melted duck fat, plus extra for sealing the jars (I like D'Artagnan brand, melted in a small saucepan over low heat)

2 tablespoons Dijon mustard

Salt and freshly ground black pepper

In a small bowl, mix together the salt, sugar, thyme, rosemary, and orange zest. Place the duck legs in a sealable plastic bag and add the spice mixture. Rub the mixture onto the duck legs, coating them completely. Seal the bag and place it in the refrigerator to cure overnight.

Preheat the oven to 300°F.

Remove the duck legs from the bag and pat most of the spice mixture off with a paper towel. Let the duck legs come to room temperature, about 15 minutes.

Heat a Dutch oven over medium-high heat and sear the duck legs skin side down. When you see the fat begin to release, about 2 to 3 minutes, lower the heat to medium-low and let the duck continue to release its fat for about 10 minutes, until the skin begins to turn golden, taking care not to burn the skin. Flip the duck legs, stir in the shallots and garlic, and sear for 3 to 5 minutes, until browned on the other side. Add the wine and orange juice and cook for another 10 minutes. Add enough chicken stock to the pot to cover the duck legs. Cover, transfer to the oven, and braise for 2 to 3 hours, checking after 2 hours, until tender when pierced with a fork and falling off the bone.

Remove the duck legs from the broth and cool enough so they can be handled. Pick the meat off the bone with a fork and place it in a food processor. With the machine running, pour in the duck fat in a thin stream and process to form a rough paste. Add the mustard, season with salt and pepper, and pulse a few times to incorporate. Transfer the mixture to the sterilized jars, cover the surface with more duck fat, and seal with the lid. The rillette will keep for up to 1 month in the refrigerator. Bring to room temperature before serving. It's best served spread over fresh baguette slices.

Pickled Cauliflower

Makes 3 cups

Cauliflower is a wonderful pickling vegetable because it holds its shape and texture well in the vinegar brine. Weeks will pass and there will still be a tangy crunch waiting for you in the jar. That said, this recipe serves as a great base for any quick pickle; feel free to throw in different vegetables—carrots, green beans, bell peppers, and okra are lovely additions.

SPECIAL EQUIPMENT: *One 64-ounce canning jar, sterilized*

3 cups distilled white vinegar

1 cup sugar

6 red chiles

2 tablespoons kosher salt

3 cups cauliflower florets cut into 1½- to 2-inch pieces

In a large saucepan, combine the vinegar, sugar, chiles, and salt and bring to a boil over medium-high heat.

Pack the cauliflower into the sterilized canning jar and pour the hot vinegar over it. Let cool to room temperature, then cover and refrigerate for at least 2 days before eating. The pickled cauliflower will keep for up to 2 weeks in the refrigerator.

Seared Scallops *and*
Chanterelle Pasta

Serves 4

Chanterelles, an autumn treasure, have a slight finish of pepper on the tongue and a smell of apricots. With their fruity and woody flavors, these mushrooms are excellent in pasta dishes, and their tulip shape makes them a beautiful addition to the plate. Scallops are lovely here too, as they lend a delicacy to the earthiness of the chanterelles.

Chanterelles are just one of an incredible variety of wild mushrooms. In the autumn months, when you see wild mushrooms begin to pop up at the market, explore the different varieties. Morels with their spongy cones absorb flavors from sauces wonderfully. And king trumpets sliced and sautéed in butter are splendid as a main course. Or if you're curious to forage your own, find an expert guide and go picking for them in early fall, right after the first rain.

4 tablespoons extra virgin olive oil

8 ounces fresh chanterelle mushrooms, cleaned and roughly torn lengthwise

Finely grated zest and juice of 1 lemon

2 garlic cloves, minced

Salt and freshly ground black pepper

¼ cup dry white wine

¼ cup heavy cream

1 pound large sea scallops (about 16)

2 tablespoons unsalted butter, cut into cubes

1 pound linguini pasta

2 tablespoons chopped fresh parsley

Bring a large pot of generously salted water to a boil.

Meanwhile, heat 2 tablespoons of the olive oil in a medium skillet over high heat until almost smoking. Add the mushrooms and sauté for 2 to 3 minutes, until softened and browned. Lower the heat to medium, add the lemon juice and garlic, and cook for an additional 2 minutes. Season with salt and pepper, transfer

to a bowl, and set aside. Keeping the heat at medium, add the wine and stir with a wooden spoon to loosen up the mushroom bits from the bottom of the skillet. Add the cream and cook to reduce the liquid for 5 to 10 minutes, stirring occasionally, until it has a sauce-like consistency. Remove from the heat and cover.

Rinse the scallops under cold water and pat them very dry with paper towels. (Drying the scallops will enable them to form a better crust while searing.) In a large non-stick skillet, heat the remaining 2 tablespoons olive oil over medium-high heat. Add the scallops in several batches and sear for 2 minutes on each side. Finish each batch by adding a couple cubes of butter to the pan, letting it melt and stirring to coat the scallops. Remove the scallops from the skillet and set aside. Cover loosely to keep warm.

Add the pasta to the boiling water and cook according to the package instructions for al dente. We like to take our pasta out 1 to 2 minutes early so that it stays firm to the bite after it's finished in the pan. Drain the pasta, reserving 1 cup of the starchy cooking water. Transfer the pasta to the pan with the sauce and warm the pasta in the sauce over medium heat. If the sauce needs loosening up, mix in a scant ¼ cup cooking water or more as needed. Add the mushrooms to the pan and toss with the pasta, then finish with the parsley and lemon zest. Season with salt and pepper. Divide the pasta among 4 plates and top each with the scallops. Serve immediately.

How to Clean

MUSHROOMS

TO CLEAN MUSHROOMS, use a mushroom brush or toothbrush to whisk away any surface dirt. To clean smaller particles of dirt trapped in the gills on the underside of the cap, brush the mushrooms under running water. Blot with a paper towel to dry.

Pomegranate Poached Figs

Serves 4

Both figs and pomegranates were some of the earliest fruits recognized and culti-
vated by humans. In Greek mythology the ruby-colored seeds of the pomegranate
were even used to tempt a goddess. Fig trees were sacred in ancient Cyprus and
have long been a symbol of fertility and sweetness. Our dessert is inspired by the
rich history and beauty of these fruits.

To poach a fig, all that is needed is a little bit of spice, a splash of liquor, and
a touch of something sweet. If you are in a pinch for time, this recipe is dessert in
minutes, though its elegance belies it. To achieve the tastiest results, work with figs
that are ripe and ready for slicing. Figs have a short season in early summer and a
second season that stretches from late summer to fall. Ripe figs should give slightly
to pressure but shouldn't be extremely soft or mushy.

½ cup crème fraîche

¼ cup plus 1 tablespoon sugar

2 cups pomegranate juice

2 tablespoons pomegranate molasses

2 tablespoons Grand Marnier

1 whole star anise

1 cinnamon stick

Finely grated zest of 1 orange

8 figs, cut in half lengthwise

Pomegranate seeds for garnish

In a small bowl, mix the crème fraîche with 1 tablespoon of the sugar and set aside.

In a medium saucepan, whisk together the pomegranate juice, pomegranate molasses, Grand Marnier, and the remaining ¼ cup sugar. Add the star anise, cinnamon stick, and orange zest, place over medium heat, and bring to a simmer. Add the figs, reduce the heat to low, and poach them for 5 minutes, or until just cooked through.

Divide the figs among 4 bowls and finish each dish with a dollop of crème fraîche and a scattering of pomegranate seeds.

HARVEST CELEBRATION

⤝⤞

*T*he weather begins to turn chilly, radiators click-clack back to life, and it's the last chance to hit the farmers' market before winter steals the bounty. The latter months of autumn are a celebration of the harvest, and there's no better way to commemorate the loss of leaves than to commune around a table and feast on the season's best flavors with a gathering of friends and family.

In the rush of the holiday season, there have been times that I missed my chance to catch a plane back home to California to join my family for a traditional Thanksgiving meal. Luckily, there is always a generous friend with a big apartment who decides to host a dinner for all the lost souls. The beauty of these gatherings comes from the potluck dishes brought by guests who inherited their recipes from great-great grandmothers, far-off uncles, and old cookbooks. Foodstuffs from all over the world are passed around family style. Curries pop with toasted cumin seeds, sweet potatoes with shaved nutmeg, braises, roasts, ripe citrus, and sweet squash are cooked down to velvet. We get to taste a little bit of everything from everywhere.

To honor these celebrations, I've chosen to share recipes here that are soul warming and fit to serve a large group. Set aside a whole day in the kitchen, dive into these pages, and get wrapped up in the smells and tastes of autumn. Have your favorite people over to feast all day until you collapse on the couch with a glass of wine—it doesn't have to be Thanksgiving to celebrate. The best part of hosting is waking up the following morning to feast on leftovers for breakfast.

Arugula, Lentil, *and* Butternut Squash Salad

Serves 6 to 8

I always have a supply of arugula in the refrigerator. The delicate leaves have a peppery bite and make for an excellent base to any salad. Here I've added lentils and sweet butternut squash to highlight the earthy flavors of autumn.

FOR THE SALAD

1 butternut squash (2 to 2½ pounds), peeled, seeded, and
    cut into ¾-inch cubes

2 tablespoons extra virgin olive oil

2 tablespoons honey

Salt

1 cup French green lentils (also known as Puy lentils)

1 tablespoon unsalted butter

1 garlic clove, minced

½ teaspoon ground cumin

Freshly ground black pepper

6 ounces arugula (about 8 cups loosely packed)

FOR THE DRESSING

2 garlic cloves, peeled

3 tablespoons fresh lemon juice

Finely grated zest of 1 lemon

3 tablespoons finely minced shallots

1 heaping tablespoon Dijon mustard

1½ tablespoons white wine vinegar

½ cup extra virgin olive oil

Salt and freshly ground black pepper

Preheat the oven to 400°F. Line a baking sheet with parchment paper.

In a large bowl, toss the butternut squash with the olive oil and honey and season generously with salt. Spread the squash in a single layer on the baking sheet and roast until beginning to brown, about 15 minutes. Stir the squash and bake for an additional 5 to 10 minutes, until fork tender. Remove from the oven and set aside to cool.

Meanwhile, place the lentils in a medium saucepan and add water to cover by 2 inches. Do not salt the cooking water to ensure the lentils will stay firm to the bite. Bring to a rolling boil over high heat, then reduce the heat to low and simmer for 25 to 30 minutes, until the lentils are fully cooked but still firm. Drain and set aside. In the same pan, melt the butter over medium heat. Add the garlic and sauté until softened, 2 to 3 minutes, then return the lentils to the pan, add the cumin, and season with salt and pepper.

To make the dressing, smash the garlic to a paste on a cutting board using the side of a chef's knife. In a small bowl, whisk together the lemon juice, zest, shallots, garlic, mustard, and vinegar. Add the olive oil in a slow drizzle as you continue to whisk until the dressing has emulsified. Season with salt and pepper.

In a large bowl, toss the arugula with the dressing and top with the lentils and roasted squash. Serve immediately.

Lamb Shoulder Stuffed *with* Wild Rice *with* Pomegranate Sauce

Serves 6 to 8

I've stuffed turkey, I've stuffed pork, and I've stuffed chicken. One day, for a change of pace, I decided to stuff a lamb shoulder. The result was a dish worthy of a celebration. Lamb shoulder is made for slow cooking; its flavors deepen over time and its tenderness is worth the wait. Wild rice adds color and bite, while the pomegranate sauce lends a tartness that brings all of the components together. Call your friends and tell them to pack the red wine. Tonight you feast!

SPECIAL EQUIPMENT: *Kitchen twine*

FOR THE WILD RICE STUFFING

½ cup dried apricots, cut into ¼-inch cubes

3 cups Basic Vegetable Stock (page 26) or good-quality packaged broth

½ teaspoon salt, plus more to taste

1 cup wild rice

2 large egg whites, lightly beaten

2 tablespoons toasted pine nuts

Freshly ground black pepper

FOR THE LAMB

1 boneless lamb shoulder (3 to 4 pounds)

2 tablespoons finely chopped fresh rosemary leaves

2 tablespoons finely chopped fresh thyme leaves

2 garlic cloves, finely minced

1 teaspoon salt

1 teaspoon freshly ground black pepper

2 tablespoons extra virgin olive oil, plus extra for brushing

1 pound whole small apples

8 ounces pearl onions, peeled

FOR THE SAUCE

I cup red wine

¼ cup pomegranate syrup (available at Middle Eastern supermarkets)

½ cup (I stick) unsalted butter, cut into ½-inch cubes

Salt and freshly ground black pepper

Place the apricots in a small bowl and add hot water to cover. Set aside for about 10 minutes to soften, then drain and set aside.

Meanwhile, in a medium saucepan, combine the vegetable stock, salt, and wild rice, place over high heat, and bring to a boil. Cover, reduce the heat to maintain a steady simmer, and cook until the rice is tender, 45 to 60 minutes. Uncover, fluff with a fork, and simmer for an additional 5 minutes. Drain off any excess liquid, set aside, and let cool for several minutes to let off steam. Fold the apricots, egg whites, and pine nuts into the rice. Season with salt and pepper. Set aside and let cool to room temperature.

Preheat the oven to 350°F.

Lay the lamb shoulder flat on a cutting board. Spread the wild rice mixture over the lamb so it's I inch thick and there's a I-inch border around the edges. Roll the lamb up lengthwise and tie it tightly with kitchen twine. With a mortar and pestle, grind together the rosemary, thyme, garlic, salt, pepper, and olive oil until it forms a paste. Massage the paste into the lamb.

Place the lamb in a large Dutch oven or casserole dish and lay the apples and onions around the lamb. Brush the apples and onions with olive oil, place the dish in the oven, and roast for I¼ to I½ hours. Insert a meat thermometer into the center of the roast to determine when it's done—if you prefer your meat rare, look for a reading of 135°F; for medium it should read 145°F. Transfer the lamb, apples, and onions to a serving dish and let rest for 20 minutes.

Strain the roasting juices through a sieve into a small saucepan. Add the wine and pomegranate syrup and cook over medium heat until reduced by half, about

20 to 30 minutes, stirring occasionally. Whisk in the butter cube by cube, letting each melt into the sauce before adding the next. Season with salt and pepper and keep warm over low heat until ready to serve.

Slice the lamb shoulder, drizzle with the sauce, and serve with the apples and onions.

Sautéed Red Cabbage *with* Caramelized Oranges

Serves 6 to 8

Red cabbage, with its deep purple color, adds a punch of brightness to cold weather dishes. Great raw or cooked, this leafy biennial is one of the most versatile veggies. It is often used for slaw, and it's also wonderful with a little heat involved. In this sautéed red cabbage dish, the vinegar helps the cabbage retain its color and the orange juice gives it zing.

> 2 tablespoons extra virgin olive oil
> 1 red onion, thinly sliced
> 2 garlic cloves, minced
> 1 head red cabbage, sliced into ¼-inch ribbons
> ½ cup orange juice
> 2 tablespoons apple cider vinegar
> Salt and freshly ground black pepper
> 2 small oranges, peeled and pith cut away

Heat a large skillet over medium heat. Add the olive oil, and when hot, add the onion and garlic and sauté until just softened, about 5 minutes. Reduce the heat

How to Cut

CABBAGE

TO CUT CABBAGE, place it on a cutting board and, using a chef's knife, cut it into quarters down the center through the stem. Carefully cut away the core and discard it. Place the cabbage flat side down on the board and slice the wedges crosswise to form ¼-inch ribbons.

to medium-low, stir in the cabbage, and sauté for about 8 minutes, until slightly wilted. Pour in the orange juice and vinegar and toss to coat the cabbage. Reduce the heat to low and simmer for 10 minutes until the cabbage is tender, stirring occasionally and keeping an eye on the pan and adding a bit more juice if it looks dry. Season with salt and pepper. Transfer the cabbage to a serving dish and cover to keep warm until ready to serve.

Cut the oranges horizontally into ¼-inch-thick round slices, removing any seeds you come across. Heat a large skillet over medium-high heat; add the oranges and cook until they are caramelized, 2 to 3 minutes on both sides.

Serve the cabbage with the caramelized oranges scattered over the top.

Pear Ginger Tart

Serves 6 to 8

Open-faced tarts have a lovely rustic appearance and are utterly delicious without being fussy, and this freeform tart, which requires little effort to make, allows the fruit flavors to shine. The homemade crust is flaky and buttery and ready to be layered with your favorite fruit, like pears and apples in the fall and winter, strawberry and rhubarb in the spring, and stone fruits in the summer. The fruits will caramelize with the sugar as they bake.

  1¼ cups all-purpose flour, plus more for dusting

  ¼ teaspoon salt

  ½ cup sugar, plus 2 tablespoons for dusting

  10 tablespoons (1¼ sticks) cold unsalted butter, cut into chunks, plus 1 tablespoon sliced

  ¼ cup cold water

  3 large Anjou pears, peeled, cored, and cut lengthwise into ¼-inch-thick slices

  1 tablespoon grated fresh ginger

  1 large egg, lightly beaten

  ¼ cup strained apricot jam, warmed

Combine the flour, salt, ½ cup of the sugar, and the butter chunks in a food processor. Pulse for about 10 seconds, until the butter is broken into pea-size pieces. Sprinkle with the cold water and pulse for another 5 seconds, just enough to combine the water with the flour mixture. On a lightly floured work surface, knead the dough just enough to bind the ingredients; avoid overworking, as it will result in a tough crust. Form the dough into a disk, cover with plastic wrap, and refrigerate for at least 1 hour. The dough can be made up to 2 days in advance.

Preheat the oven to 400°F. Line a baking sheet with parchment paper.

On a lightly floured work surface, roll the dough into a 14-inch round. Gently transfer the dough onto the prepared baking sheet. Arrange the pear slices, slightly overlapping, in a spiral starting from the center of the dough to within 2 inches of the edge. Fold the overhanging dough over the fruit. Sprinkle the grated ginger and the remaining 2 tablespoons sugar over the exposed pears, then top with remaining butter slices. Brush the edges of dough with the beaten egg.

Bake the tart until the pears are caramelized and the crust is golden brown and flaky, 40 to 50 minutes. Transfer the tart to a wire rack and brush the pears with the apricot jam. Let cool slightly before serving.

COOKIE MONSTER

⤜⤛

I can never eat just one cookie. From the moment the butter and sugar are creamed, I have to consciously retain myself from sticking a pinky into the mixture and testing the sweet cream for texture, or flavor, or saltiness, anything that grants me the excuse to dig in to the whirl of sugar prematurely. The importance of tasting a recipe along its way to fruition is good cooking practice anyway, right? This is especially important with cookies.

The nutty smell of butter melting into sugar and the slight heat escaping outside of the warmed oven peaks my anticipation, challenges my patience, and spikes my hunger. I can hardly wait to pinch off a piece of still-warm dough from the baking sheet when the kitchen buzzer breaks its silence.

Cookie baking is in its own realm of confections, as cookies are more than tasty morsels. When bitten into, a surge of warmth and comfort billows inside of us, like the smell of fresh coffee first thing in the morning. The aroma seeps into everything: clothes, far-off rooms, the linens, the furniture—and the home is better for it. Cookies are communal, and whether they are sweet or savory, soft or with a slight crunch, called biscuits or crumpets, they always hit the spot and are even better when shared with a companion.

Over the years I've embraced my inner cookie monster. The ritual of baking a batch of dough into tiny sweet treats is one I indulge in more often than I used to. I'm not ashamed to admit that when the pan arrives hot out of the oven, I scoop in almost immediately for a bite of a too-warm-to-actually-taste, still-melting-in-the-pan cookie. But nothing makes me happier than just that moment.

The following is my favorite collection of cookies that hits every spot.

Art Deco Cookies

Makes about 2 dozen cookies

If cookies could tell a story, these would tell the tale of a couple of ladies coming of age. Inspired by our original Jewel cookies, these edible faceted gems are an updated, simplified version of our past cookie. We stayed true to the geometric shapes of the original but added a little bit of wisdom we've acquired over the years—less icing, more texture! To nail a fully dimensional cookie, stack two different shapes of dough on top of each other before baking. Gather a variety of sanding sugars and food coloring, and tell your own story through these tiny works of art.

SPECIAL EQUIPMENT: *Assorted geometric-shaped cookie cutters*

3 cups all-purpose flour, plus more for the work surface

½ teaspoon baking powder

¼ teaspoon salt

1 cup granulated sugar

1 cup (2 sticks) unsalted butter, softened

1 large egg

1 teaspoon vanilla extract

Royal Icing (see sidebar)

Food coloring in assorted colors

Colored sanding sugars (I like India Tree brand)

White sugar pearls for decorating (I like Wilton brand)

Silver dragees for decorating

In a large bowl, whisk together the flour, baking powder, and salt.

Using an electric mixer on medium speed, beat the granulated sugar with the butter until pale and fluffy, about 3 minutes. Add the egg and vanilla and mix until well combined. With the mixer on low speed, slowly add the flour mixture,

and mix until a dough forms. Turn the dough out onto a work surface and divide it into quarters. Form each quarter into a 5-inch disk. Wrap each disk with plastic wrap and refrigerate until firm, about 2 hours.

Preheat the oven to 350°F.

On a lightly floured work surface, roll out the dough to ¼ inch thick. Using the geometric-shaped cookie cutters, cut out whatever shapes you like and transfer them to 2 parchment-lined baking sheets. Leave at least 1 inch space between the cookies. Bake until the edges are golden brown, 7 to 10 minutes. Transfer the cookies to a wire rack and let them cool completely.

Decorate the cookies using the Royal Icing (see below), sanding sugars, sugar pearls, and dragees.

How to Make

ROYAL ICING

Makes 3 cups

1 box confectioner's sugar (1 pound), 2 large egg whites, ½ teaspoon vanilla extract.

IN THE LARGE BOWL of an electric mixer, combine the egg whites and vanilla and beat until frothy. Slowly mix in the confectioners' sugar and mix on low speed until the sugar is incorporated and the mixture is glossy. Increase the speed to high and beat until the mixture forms stiff peaks, about 5 minutes. For a thinner consistency, add water one tablespoon at a time. Separate the mixture into small bowls and add food coloring as desired. The icing can be stored in the refrigerator in an airtight container for up to 3 days.

When you're ready to apply the icing, transfer each colored icing to a disposable pastry bag fitted with a round tip (such as Wilton No. 3).

Raspberry Lychee Sables

Makes about 3 dozen cookies

Sables are classically French and universally delicious. The cookie itself is buttery with a slight flakiness and serves as an ideal vessel for whatever flavor you desire to tuck inside. For this version, I've made a jam with raspberry and lychee, but feel free to use whatever jam you fancy. These cookies are fantastic with a cup of afternoon tea or served alongside champagne and a small fete of friends.

SPECIAL EQUIPMENT: *1½-inch fluted round cookie cutter*

1 cup (2 sticks) unsalted butter, softened

¼ teaspoon salt

1 large egg

1 teaspoon vanilla extract

⅓ cup granulated sugar

¼ cup confectioners' sugar, plus more for dusting

2 cups all-purpose flour

Raspberry Lychee Jam (see sidebar)

In a large bowl, using an electric mixer on medium speed, beat the butter until smooth and creamy, about 2 minutes. Mix in the salt, egg, and vanilla extract. With the mixer on low speed, slowly add the sugars and mix until smooth, about 1 minute. Slowly add the flour and mix until just combined.

Turn the dough out onto a work surface and divide it into half. Form each half into a 6-inch disk. Wrap each disk with plastic wrap and refrigerate until firm, about 2 hours.

Preheat the oven to 350°F.

On a lightly floured work surface, roll out the dough to ¼ inch thick. Using the cookie cutter, cut out the tops and bottoms and transfer to 2 parchment-lined baking sheets. Leave at least 1 inch between the cookies. Transfer the cookies to the oven and bake until the edges are golden brown, about 15 to 20 minutes. Transfer the cookies to a wire rack and let them cool completely.

Fill each cookie with Raspberry Lychee Jam and dust the tops with confectioners' sugar.

How to Make

RASBERRY LYCHEE JAM

Makes about 2 cups

1 can lychees, drained; 1 (10-ounce) jar raspberry jam.

PLACE THE LYCHEES in the bowl of a food processor and process until smooth. Transfer the lychees to a medium saucepan along with the raspberry jam. Cook, stirring occasionally, over medium-high heat until the jam mixture has reduced and thickened, about 20 minutes. Remove it from the heat and let it cool. Transfer it to an airtight container until ready to use. You can make it ahead of time and store it in the refrigerator for up to 3 days.

Fig Walnut Oatmeal Cookies

Makes about 2 dozen cookies

There's something about the chew of an oatmeal cookie. They are tender, and their sweetness never cloys. For this recipe, I've included figs for a bit of subtle sweetness, and walnuts for a boost of crunch. When taken out of the oven, the toasted oats and the roasted walnuts together smell like browned butter. These morsels are delicious straight off the cooling rack, with a scoop of ice cream, or for breakfast the next morning.

I cup all-purpose flour

½ teaspoon baking powder

¼ teaspoon baking soda

½ teaspoon ground cinnamon

¼ teaspoon nutmeg

Pinch of salt

½ cup (I stick) unsalted butter, softened

⅔ cup packed light-brown sugar

⅓ cup granulated sugar

I large egg

I teaspoon vanilla extract

1½ cups old-fashioned rolled oats

½ cup dried Mission figs, stems discarded, chopped

½ cup walnuts, chopped

Preheat the oven to 350°F.

In a large bowl, mix together the flour, baking powder, baking soda, cinnamon, nutmeg, and salt. In another bowl, using an electric mixer on medium speed, beat the butter and sugars until pale and fluffy. Add the egg and vanilla to the mixture. Gradually mix in the flour mixture and oats. Gently fold the figs and walnuts into the mixture.

Drop the dough by the spoonful onto parchment-lined baking sheets, leaving a 2-inch space between cookies. Bake until the edges are golden, about 15 to 18 minutes. Transfer the cookies to a wire cooling rack. The cookies can be stored in an airtight container for up to 5 days.

Flourless Chocolate Caramel Cookies

Makes about a dozen cookies

Rich, decadent, and moist, these flourless cookies are the answer to any and all chocolate cravings. This recipe is a simple one to make and will have everyone who partakes begging for more. These cookies demand to be eaten straight out of the oven, when the caramel is still warm and gooey.

SPECIAL EQUIPMENT: *1½-inch cookie scoop (optional)*

2 cups confectioners' sugar

1 cup unsweetened cocoa powder (I like Valrhona brand)

¼ teaspoon salt

½ teaspoon baking powder

3 large egg whites, at room temperature

1 teaspoon vanilla extract

6 caramel squares, halved

Preheat the oven to 350°F.

In a large bowl, using an electric mixer on low speed, combine the confectioners' sugar, cocoa powder, salt, and baking powder. Increase the speed to medium and add the egg whites and vanilla extract. Beat until the batter just comes together, but do not overbeat.

Shape the caramel halves into small discs. With the cookie scoop or a spoon, scoop the batter and press a caramel disc into the center before dropping it onto a parchment-lined baking sheet. Leave 2 inches between each cookie. Bake for 10 to 12 minutes, until the tops are cracked and glossy. Transfer the cookies to a wire cooling rack. The cookies can be stored in an airtight container for up to 5 days.

WINTER

Chill air and wintry winds!

My ear has grown familiar with your song;

I hear it in the opening year,

I listen, and it cheers me long.

HENRY WADSWORTH LONGFELLOW

SNOW DAY

⤜⤛

The first time I saw "snow" I was in elementary school, when for one day our Southern California schoolyard was transformed into a winter wonderland. Buckets and barrels of shaved ice from snow machines were dropped all over, and like savages we plundered through the half-melting faux flurries, careless and wild. By afternoon it was over. Half-built snowmen began their slow melt under the heat of the sun, but it was magical while it lasted.

In New York the first flurries of the season never fail to bring me back to that schoolyard full of snow. The shuffle and hustle of the crowds turns quiet and the city slows down. The first snow day is a welcome retreat and holds the promise of a day free of worries.

Mealtime is loosely defined on wintry days. Rather than sitting down for three square meals, snacking becomes an all-day activity. I find warmth inside my apartment from the steam that rises from a mug of hot chocolate, a comforting bite to eat, and a game of cards or a stack of books and magazines I've been meaning to read. Fuzzy socks and my favorite sweater are my preferred outfit. The recipes that follow are comfort foods perfect for a morning, afternoon, or evening of hibernation.

Hazelnut Hot Chocolate

Serves 4

Hot chocolate is soul food—warming for both body and mind. And when it's cold outside, it is my go-to beverage, the perfect chilly weather treat. To add richness and a good amount of depth, I've added a touch of Nutella for its dreamy hazelnut flavor, and to finish, I top it off with a generous serving of freshly whipped cream.

FOR THE WHIPPED CREAM

½ cup heavy cream, chilled

I tablespoon confectioners' sugar

½ teaspoon vanilla extract

FOR THE HOT CHOCOLATE

¼ cup sugar

⅓ cup unsweetened cocoa powder, plus extra for finishing

Pinch of salt

4 cups milk

¼ cup Nutella

½ teaspoon vanilla extract

To make the whipped cream, pour the chilled heavy cream into a bowl and add the confectioners' sugar and vanilla. Using an electric mixer or whisk, beat the cream into soft peaks; do not overbeat. The cream can be made ahead of time and kept covered in the refrigerator for up to I day.

To make the hot chocolate, combine the sugar, cocoa powder, and salt in a small bowl. In a medium saucepan, heat the milk over medium-low heat until it starts to simmer. Whisk in the Nutella until well combined, then slowly add cocoa mixture, whisking until smooth. Stir in the vanilla.

To serve, pour the cocoa into 4 mugs and top each off with whipped cream and a dusting of cocoa powder.

Sweet *and* Salty Kettle Corn

Serves 4 (or just 1)

Put in a movie you've seen a million times and sink you fingers deep into a bowl of just-popped kettle corn. Enjoy the sweet and salty crunchiness of it. I usually eat the entire bowl so quickly that I have to pause the movie halfway through to make another big batch.

    ¼ cup canola oil
    ½ cup popcorn kernels
    ¼ cup sugar
    1 teaspoon ground cinnamon
    Salt

In a large pot, heat the oil over medium-high heat. Add 2 or 3 popcorn kernels and put the lid on. When you hear the kernels begin to pop, take the pot off the heat and stir in the rest of the kernels along with the sugar. Place the lid back on and put the pot back on the stove. Shake the pot as the popcorn pops, continuing to shake until the popping slows down, about 3 minutes. Remove from the heat and pour the popcorn into a large bowl. Toss in the cinnamon and season with salt.

Roasted Tomato *and* Garlic Soup

Serves 4 to 6

In the winter, many days all I want is a big bowl of soup, and this soup brings a taste of sunshine to the cold-weather months. I usually double the recipe so I can eat it for an entire week, heating it up anytime I'm craving some warmth. Roasting canned tomatoes and garlic gives this simple soup complexity of flavor—a slight nuttiness from the bits that get charred and a mellow sweetness that develops from its time in the oven.

1 head garlic

¼ cup plus 2 tablespoons extra virgin olive oil, plus extra for brushing

One 35-ounce can whole peeled tomatoes, drained and halved
    (we like Cento brand)

Salt and freshly ground black pepper

2 small onions, diced

1 quart Homemade Chicken Stock (page 93) or Basic Vegetable Stock
    (page 26) (or substitute a good-quality packaged broth)

2 tablespoons unsalted butter

1 cup chopped fresh basil leaves

Preheat the oven to 400°F.

Peel away a few of the outer layers of the garlic bulb skin, leaving the cloves intact. Cut the top off the head of garlic, exposing a bit of each of the individual cloves. Brush the exposed garlic with olive oil, wrap the bulb tightly in aluminum foil, and place on a baking sheet.

On another baking sheet, toss the tomatoes with ¼ cup of the olive oil and spread them out in a single layer. Season generously with salt and pepper.

Place both pans in the oven to roast for 30 to 35 minutes, until the garlic is soft and the tomatoes are caramelized. Remove from the oven and set aside until the garlic is cool enough to handle. Squeeze the roasted garlic out of each clove; reserve in a dish.

Meanwhile, heat the remaining 2 tablespoons olive oil in a large saucepan over medium heat. Add the onions and sauté until golden and softened, about 10 minutes. Add the tomatoes, garlic, stock, and butter. Bring to a gentle boil, then adjust the heat and simmer uncovered for 30 minutes. Add the basil and puree the soup in batches in a blender or using an immersion blender until smooth. Season with salt and pepper and serve.

How to Make
Homemade
CHICKEN STOCK

Makes about 2 quarts

4 pounds assorted chicken parts (backs, necks, legs, and wings); 2 onions, quartered; 2 celery stalks, cut into 2-inch pieces; 2 large carrots, cut into 2-inch pieces; 6 large garlic cloves, crushed; 3 sprigs fresh thyme; 3 sprigs fresh flat-leaf parlsey; 1 bay leaf; 1 teaspoon whole black peppercorns; 3 quarts water.

COMBINE ALL INGREDIENTS with 3 quarts of water in a large stockpot. Bring to a boil over medium-high heat; reduce heat and simmer gently for 2½ hours or until stock is reduced to about 8 cups. Using a ladle, skim the impurities and fat that rise to the surface.

Remove from heat and strain stock through a fine sieve and discard solids. Once cooled, stock can be stored covered in the refrigerator for 3 days or frozen for up to 3 months.

Double Grilled Cheese *and* Ham Sandwiches

Serves 4

Why not put the cheese in a grilled cheese on the outside of the bread? This was my revelation while making my usual grilled cheese over the stove and snacking on some of the crunchy cheese bits that had fallen off to the side of the pan. The cheese melts down to form a crisp crust on the outside of the bread while keeping the insides soft and gooey. You can leave out the ham and swap in leafy kale for a vegetarian version. Serve with tomato soup (see my recipe on page 92), a classic combo that warms you up on cold weather days.

1½ cups grated sharp cheddar cheese

1½ cups grated Gruyère or Comté cheese

8 slices white sandwich bread

6 tablespoons unsalted butter, softened

4 slices smoked ham

Preheat the oven to 200°F.

In a medium bowl, combine the cheddar and Gruyère cheeses.

Generously butter one side of each slice of bread. Heat a large nonstick skillet over medium-low heat and scatter ¼ cup of the shredded cheese onto the skillet. Place a slice of bread, buttered side down, in the skillet on top of the cheese. Cover the bread with ¼ cup of the shredded cheese, a slice of ham, and a second slice of bread. Cook until golden underneath, about 2 minutes. Lift the sandwich off the pan with spatula and scatter another ¼ cup of shredded cheese onto the pan. Flip the sandwich over, place it back in the pan on top of the cheese, and cook for another 2 minutes, or until the cheese is golden and crisp. Repeat with the remaining ingredients to make 4 sandwiches. Keep the finished sandwiches warm in the oven on a baking sheet until they are all done. Serve while hot and gooey.

PANTRY COOKING

᚛⸝

The pantry is a cook's best-kept secret, an extension of oneself. Walking into someone's pantry is as intimate as opening their closet. The treasures inside paint a picture. In my pantry there's the truffle oil a friend gave me as a gift from La Maison de la Truffe in Paris that I can never bring myself to drizzle—it seems too special, a mix of Indian spices hoarded from many trips to Kalustyan's Indian grocery store in New York City, filling grains, speckled heirloom beans, and colorful cans of sardines I brought back from Spain that are perfect for topping on crackers.

My first winter on the East Coast was so cold and windy that I could barely bring myself to step foot outside, even for food. One particularly chilly day I put on layers of clothing, threw on my jacket—more like a sleeping bag with arm holes—and dashed across the street to the corner grocery store. I quickly planned my dinner on the spot, grabbing a protein and a couple of ingredients that I could use in a handful of ways.

As I stepped back into my apartment, I peeked into my pantry and felt relief at the sight of foods that I had been slowly squirreling away all year. My little bunker saved the day. Having a well-stocked pantry with a balance of grains, legumes, flours, and spices makes all the difference, enabling to me create meals anytime. That day I dipped into my reserve and pulled from the shelves a box of risotto, heirloom beans, big bars of Valrhona chocolate, and root vegetables and improvised a meal on a whim. Whatever I decide to use out of the pantry, the outcomes are always comforting and satisfying. This chapter includes a collection of ideas to inspire you to get creative with your own pantry for those days when the snow keeps you trapped indoors.

Tomatoes ☐	Artichokes ☐	Olives & Capers ☐	Oil-Packed Tuna ☐	Chicken Broth ☐
Assorted Pasta ☐	Flour ☐	Grains ☐	Legumes ☐	Nuts ☐
Potatoes ☐	Onions ☐	*The* WELL-STOCKED PANTRY *a* BASIC CHECKLIST	Garlic ☐	Lemons ☐
White Wine ☐	Olive Oil ☐	Vinegar ☐	Soy Sauce ☐	Herbs ☐
Spices ☐	Anchovies ☐	Dijon Mustard ☐	Dried Mushrooms ☐	Baking Chocolate ☐

Canned Items — *Dry Goods* — *Produce* — *Condiments & Flavorings*

Key: ■ CANNED ITEMS ■ DRY GOODS ■ PRODUCE ■ CONDIMENTS & FLAVORINGS

Chart No. 002

Heirloom Bean Soup *with* Crispy Kale

Serves 4 to 6

Heirloom beans, in a variety of shapes and sizes, a rainbow of colors, and speckled patterns, are almost too beautiful to cook. These beans are often found through seed banks—organizations that save seeds from extinction and contamination. There's been a resurgence of nearly extinct bean varieties in recent years, and I've been happily experimenting with them. My favorites come from Rancho Gordo located in Napa, California, and can be bought at natural and specialty food markets or ordered online. I love great Northern beans in this recipe, but any white heirloom or more commonly found cannellini can be used.

8 ounces dried white heirloom beans

1 bunch kale

¼ cup plus 2 tablespoons extra virgin olive oil

Salt and freshly ground black pepper

2 shallots, thinly sliced

2 garlic cloves, minced

Splash of dry white wine

1 quart Basic Vegetable Stock (page 26) or good-quality packaged broth

1 bay leaf

Parsley Oil (recipe follows)

CRISPY KALE

CRISPY KALE CHIPS make a great healthy snack on their own. Feel free to experiment with different toppings such as grated Parmesan cheese, soy sauce and sesame seeds, Herbes de Provence, or lime juice and chili powder.

Place the beans in a bowl, add water to cover by a few inches, and soak the beans for at least 6 hours or overnight. Drain and set aside.

Preheat the oven to 300°F. Line a baking sheet with parchment paper.

Wash and thoroughly dry the kale. Remove the stems from the kale and tear the leaves into large pieces. Toss with ¼ cup of the olive oil, season with salt and pepper, and arrange in a single layer on the prepared baking sheet. Roast until darkened a bit and crisp, about 20 minutes, tossing occasionally and taking care not to let it burn. Remove from the oven and set aside.

Heat the remaining 2 tablespoons olive oil in a large saucepan over medium heat. Add the shallots and sauté until translucent, about 3 minutes. Stir in the garlic and cook for another 2 minutes, or until softened. Splash a bit of white wine into the pot and use a wooden spoon to loosen up any bits stuck to the bottom. Add the beans, vegetable stock, and bay leaf, bring to a boil, then reduce the heat and simmer gently for 40 to 50 minutes, until the beans are cooked through. Remove the bay leaf.

Remove a cup or so of beans with a slotted spoon and set aside. Puree the soup in batches in a blender or using an immersion blender until smooth. Season with salt and pepper. To serve, ladle the soup into bowls and top each with some whole beans, crisp kale, and a drizzle of parsley oil.

How to Make

PARSLEY OIL

PARSLEY OIL CAN ALSO BE TOSSED with pasta dishes, made into salad dressing by adding a dash of vinegar, or used to make chimichurri sauce by adding minced garlic cloves and lemon to serve with grilled meats.

Makes ¼ cup

¼ cup extra virgin olive oil, ½ cup lightly packed fresh parsley leaves, salt and freshly ground black pepper.

In a mini food processor, pulse the olive oil with the parsley until it has a smooth consistency. Transfer to a bowl, season with salt and pepper, and set aside until ready to use.

Wild Mushroom Risotto *with* Caramelized Leeks

Serves 4 to 6

Building a proper pantry is not done without a stash of rice. Some of the varieties I keep on hand are long-grain aromatic basmati rice, jasmine rice, nutty wild rice, and everyday brown rice. And I always have a box or two of Arborio waiting for the days when I crave a creamy risotto. There's something soothing about the continuous stirring and slow addition of broth while leaning over a hot stove that makes this dish a wintertime favorite for me—it's both warming to make and warming to eat.

I quart Homemade Chicken Stock (page 93)or Basic Vegetable Stock (page 26)
   (or substitute a good-quality packaged broth)
2 tablespoons extra virgin olive oil, plus more for drizzling
2 shallots, finely chopped
I leek, white and light green parts, tough outer leaves discarded, sliced into
   ¼-inch-thick rounds
I¼ cups Arborio rice
⅓ cup white wine
2 large handfuls shiitake or wild mushrooms, thinly sliced
2 tablespoons unsalted butter
½ cup freshly grated Parmesan cheese
2 tablespoons roughly chopped fresh parsley
Salt and freshly ground black pepper

In a medium saucepan, bring the stock to a simmer and keep it at a low simmer.

In a large saucepan, heat the olive oil over medium heat. Add the shallots and leek and cook for 10 to 15 minutes, until the leeks are caramelized. Increase the heat, stir in the rice, then add the wine. Keep stirring until the liquid is absorbed. Pour in a ladle of hot stock and turn the heat down to a simmer. Stir continuously,

adding a ladle of stock at a time and allowing each ladleful to be absorbed before adding the next. Continue adding stock until the rice is cooked but still al dente, about 30 minutes.

Meanwhile, preheat the oven to 400°F. Line a baking sheet with parchment paper.

Scatter the mushrooms in a single layer on the prepared baking sheet. Drizzle with olive oil and generously season with salt and pepper. Roast until golden and crisp, 15 to 20 minutes, checking every 5 minutes and tossing to avoid burning the edges. Remove from the oven and set aside.

Take the risotto off the heat and stir in the butter, cheese, and parsley. It should have a creamy consistency; if not add a little more stock. Season with salt and pepper.

Divide the risotto among bowls and top each with roasted mushrooms and a drizzle of olive oil.

Duck Sausage *with* Potatoes *and* Crispy Shallots

Serves 6

This meal is simple and ultra-comforting. Potatoes are a pantry staple, and sausages can be stowed away in the freezer for impromptu use. In this dish, the potatoes are boiled and smashed before frying them, resulting in a tender interior and deliciously crispy crust. Whip this up when time has slipped away from you but your appetite hasn't. If you're feeling virtuous, serve it with a green salad to round out the meal.

Salt

1½ pounds unpeeled small baby red or yellow potatoes

¼ cup extra virgin olive oil

2 shallots, thinly sliced

6 duck sausages

3 tablespoons plum or cherry preserves

2 tablespoons balsamic vinegar

2 tablespoons soy sauce

Bring a medium pot of salted water to boil over medium-high heat. Add the potatoes and boil until cooked through, about 10 minutes. Drain the potatoes and set aside.

Heat the olive oil in a cast-iron pan over medium heat until the oil shimmers or reaches 325°F as measured on an instant-read thermometer. Add the shallots and fry until golden brown, 1 to 1½ minutes, taking care not to burn them. Remove the shallots with a slotted spoon and transfer to a paper towel–lined plate. Reserve the oil in the pan for frying the potatoes.

Place the potatoes on a work surface, cover with parchment paper, and smash them lightly with a potato masher or the bottom of a heavy pan. Reheat the olive oil in the same pan over medium heat, add the potatoes, and fry until they are crisp on the outside, 2 to 3 minutes. Remove with a slotted spoon and set aside on a paper towel–lined baking sheet.

In the same pan with the remaining oil, add the sausages and cook until browned and cooked through, about 5 minutes per side. Remove the sausages and place on the baking sheet along with the potatoes. Pour out any remaining oil from pan.

In a small bowl, mix together the preserves, vinegar, and soy sauce until smooth. Add the preserve mixture to the pan and warm the sauce over medium-low heat. To serve, divide the sausages and potatoes among plates, drizzle with the sauce, and top with crispy shallots.

Chocolate Pots de Crème *with* Jasmine Honey Cream

Serves 6

Pots de crème are equal parts rich and creamy. I love to add a little something floral to the custard to give the classic flavors another layer of complexity. Here I've opted for a hint of jasmine and honey, lending a delicate finish that balances out the richness of this dessert. These are simple to make but need time to chill—I recommend making them a day in advance, then whipping the cream just before serving.

POTS DE CRÈME

7 ounces bittersweet chocolate, finely chopped, plus a
    1-ounce chunk for shavings
½ cup whole milk
1½ cups heavy cream
6 large egg yolks
1½ tablespoons sugar
Pinch of sea salt
Jasmine Honey Cream (recipe follows)

Preheat the oven to 350°F.

Place the chopped chocolate in a medium heatproof bowl. In a medium saucepan, combine the milk, heavy cream, egg yolks, sugar, and salt. Place over low heat and bring to a simmer; simmer, whisking constantly, until the sugar has dissolved and the mixture has thickened enough to coat a spoon, 5 to 6 minutes. Pour the custard over the chocolate in a slow steady stream, continuously whisking until the chocolate has melted. Pour the mixture through a fine-mesh sieve, straining out any solids. Divide the custard among 6 ovenproof ramekins and cover each tightly

with foil. With a toothpick or fork, poke several holes in the foil to allow steam to escape.

Set the ramekins in a baking pan and pour in hot water to reach halfway up the sides of the ramekins. Transfer the pan to the oven, taking care not to let water splash into the ramekins. Bake for 35 to 40 minutes, until the custards are set but still jiggly in the center. Remove the ramekins from the pan, loosen the foil lids (but don't remove them), and place on a wire rack to cool, then transfer to the refrigerator to chill for at least 2 hours or overnight.

Top each pot de crème with a dollop of Jasmine Honey Cream (recipe follows). Using a vegetable peeler, slowly shave the side of the remaining 1 ounce chocolate to create thin, flat shavings and sprinkle them over the pots de crème.

JASMINE HONEY CREAM

1 cup heavy cream

1 tablespoon loose-leaf jasmine tea or 2 jasmine tea bags

1 tablespoon honey

In a jar, combine the heavy cream with the tea leaves. Cover and steep in the refrigerator overnight. Strain the cream into a mixing bowl, discarding the tea leaves. Add the honey and whisk by hand or with an electric mixer until soft peaks form; do not overbeat.

GLITTER AND GOLD

⊰※⊱

*E*very now and then I love to throw a big party at home. It could be as obvious as celebrating New Year's Eve or the winter solstice, but life's events can also make the perfect excuse—a friend arrives back to New York after traveling the world, I've just shaken up a new cocktail, and so on. I transform my daily living space into a glittered jewel box, lining my apartment with tinsel, draping the ceiling in garlands, and filling every room with floating balloons. It's the perfect backdrop for a night of popping champagne and dancing with friends until the sun comes up.

For these occasions I set out a long table dressed with a simple cloth. Rather than bothering with formal place settings, I like to mix and match the adornments on the table with what I already own and make the food part of the decor. From my cupboard I grab my favorite bowls and fill a couple of them high with pretty foods like Concord grapes or walnuts in their shells and leave a few empty to collect seeds and shells. Platters are filled with knobs of cheese, some wedges soft and pungent, others hard and nutty. Crostini follow suit on a copper tray I found at the flea market and oysters shimmer on shallow bowls of ice.

The tastiest hors d'oeuvres are the simplest: oysters, caviar, champagne, and little toasts with toppings. Taking advantage of store-bought items makes the party planning easier. The recipes that follow are as luxurious as they are effortless. Not only will they tantalize your taste buds and elevate the mood; they will guarantee that you spend as little time in the kitchen as possible so you'll have plenty of time to spend with your guests and dance with abandon.

Spiced Pear Prosecco Cocktail

Serves 12

This spiced cocktail is perfect for sipping at a wintertime party. Cinnamon, star anise, and cloves give the pear nectar an aromatic quality, and bubbly prosecco adds festive elegance. For an equally delicious nonalcoholic beverage, replace the bubbly with seltzer. Either version is worthy of toasting with.

I cup water

I cup sugar

3 cups pear nectar

4 star anise, plus 12 for garnish

4 cloves

2 cinnamon sticks

Two 750-ml bottles Prosecco, chilled

In a small saucepan, combine the water, sugar, pear nectar, star anise, cloves, and cinnamon sticks. Place over medium heat and bring to a boil, then reduce the heat to low and simmer for 10 minutes, or until the liquid thickens to a syrup. Remove from the heat and steep for 20 minutes for the flavors to infuse. Strain the syrup through a sieve into a jar and discard the spices. Let cool to room temperature, then cover and refrigerate until chilled, about I hour. The syrup can be made ahead of time and stored in the refrigerator for up to I week.

To make the cocktails, fill each glass with ¼ cup pear syrup, top off with Prosecco, and drop in a star anise for garnish.

Oysters *with* Cucumber Mignonette

Serves 12

With their glistening shells and pearly color, oysters are the sexiest delicacy from the sea. When brought into a room, guests swoon and become giddy. Slurped straight from the shell, they taste like the ocean, and they are particularly delicious dressed with a bright cucumber mignonette or a simple squeeze of lemon juice to bring out their briny flavor.

SPECIAL EQUIPMENT: *oyster knife*

2 cups rice vinegar

2 tablespoons fresh lime juice

1 cup peeled, seeded, and finely chopped cucumber

¼ cup finely chopped shallot

2 tablespoons finely chopped fresh dill

2 tablespoons sugar

Freshly ground black pepper

36 fresh oysters, scrubbed

Crushed ice

Seaweed for garnish (optional)

Lemon wedges for serving

In a small bowl, whisk together the vinegar, lime juice, cucumber, shallots, dill, and sugar and season with pepper. Cover and refrigerate for at least 15 minutes, or until ready to use. The mignonnette can be made the day before and stored in the refrigerator.

　To shuck the oysters, begin by readying a small towel to hold the oysters steady and to protect your hands. Place an oyster on a flat surface with the hinge side toward you. Keeping your hand secure across the oyster, insert the oyster knife through the hinge. When you feel the knife slide between the shell, twist until the hinge pops open. Loosen any muscle attached to the meat with the knife and detach the oyster from the top shell. Remove any shell bits. Place the oyster in its half shell along with its natural juices over a bed of crushed ice and seaweed. Repeat with the remaining oysters. Serve immediately with the cucumber mignonnette and lemon wedges on the side.

Flavors of the OYSTER

EVERYONE HAS THEIR PREFERENCES when it comes to oysters. Some like bold oysters that have a brassy lemon finish, while others enjoy petite oysters with a creamy and mild finish. For the most part, the larger the oyster, the more intense and saline the flavor. I grew up eating small Kumamotos with their delicate creamy melon flavors and sharp fluted shells. If you like your oysters on the sweeter side, you may also want to try the Totten Inlets from Washington and Hog Island Sweetwaters from California. When I moved to the East Coast I began eating larger oysters with brinier flavors such as Blue Points, Wellfleets, and wild Malpeques. Beausoleils from New Brunswick, Canada, provide a nice balance of delicate refined flavors with a briny finish.

Mixed Crostini

Serves a crowd (about 30 slices of each variety)

With a variety of toppings that combine savory and sweet flavors, these toasty slices of bread make the perfect finger food, and preparing several types of crostini ahead of time ensures your guests will have plenty to snack on. Feel free to experiment with any jams or other toppings you have in the fridge. The components are easy to prep ahead of time, and crostini taste best when assembled right before serving.

CROSTINI

3 baguettes, cut diagonally into ½-inch slices

Extra virgin olive oil for brushing

Salt and freshly ground black pepper

Preheat the oven to 400°F. Line a baking sheet with parchment paper.

Lightly brush one side of each bread slice with olive oil and sprinkle with salt and pepper. Place on the prepared baking sheet and toast in the oven until golden, about 5 minutes. Remove from the oven, set aside, and allow to cool on the baking sheet. Repeat in batches with the remaining bread slices.

PROSCIUTTO, PEAR, BLUE CHEESE, AND HONEY CROSTINI

8 ounces prosciutto, thinly sliced

30 slices Crostini (from 1 baguette; see instructions above)

½ pear, cored and thinly sliced

8 ounces blue cheese, preferably Saint Agur, thinly sliced

Honey for drizzling

Freshly ground black pepper

Fold the prosciutto slices and place them on top of the prepared crostini. Follow with the pear slices and blue cheese and finish with a drizzle with honey. Season with pepper.

SMOKED SABLE, WHITE BEAN HUMMUS, AND FRIED CAPER CROSTINI

15 ounces (1½ cups) cooked (or one 15-ounce can) white beans, such as cannellini, drained, liquid reserved

¼ cup tahini

Juice of 2 lemons

¼ cup plus 2 tablespoons extra virgin olive oil

2 garlic cloves, chopped

Salt and freshly ground black pepper

¼ cup small capers, drained and patted dry

30 slices Crostini (from 1 baguette; see instructions on page 122)

8 ounces smoked sable

To make the hummus: Combine the beans, tahini, lemon juice, ¼ cup of the ol-
ive oil, and the garlic in a food processor and process until smooth, adding some reserved bean liquid as needed to thin the hummus if needed. Season with salt and pepper. The hummus can be made a day in advance and kept covered in the refrigerator.

Heat the remaining 2 tablespoons olive oil in a small skillet over medium-high heat. Add the capers and cook until crisp, about 1 minute. Remove from the pan to a paper towel–lined plate.

To assemble the crostini: smear each one with white bean hummus, followed by some smoked sable and fried capers. Use any leftover hummus as a dip for veggies—carrots, radishes, celery, and cucumber make great crudités.

SPICE-RUBBED STEAK AND MANGO CHUTNEY CROSTINI

1 tablespoon brown sugar

½ teaspoon ground cumin

½ teaspoon salt

½ teaspoon garlic powder

2 tablespoons extra virgin olive oil

8 ounces flank steak, trimmed of excess fat

30 slices Crostini (from 1 baguette; see instructions on page 122)

½ cup prepared mango chutney (we like Stonewall Kitchen)

Freshly ground black pepper

In a small bowl, mix together the brown sugar, cumin, salt, garlic powder, and olive oil. Rub the mixture all over the steak and let marinate for at least 15 minutes or overnight in the refrigerator if you're prepping it in advance.

Heat a grill pan over high heat. Place the steak onto the hot grill and cook for 5 minutes on each side. Set aside and let rest for 10 minutes, then cut into thin slices. Spread the crostini with the mango chutney and top with the sliced steak. Finish with a sprinkling of pepper.

Bombe Alaska *with* Cherry Chocolate Chip Ice Cream

Serves 10 to 12

Here's what I remember of my first fine dining experience as child: At the end of dinner, our server rolled out a fancy cart covered in tiered desserts. My eyes lit up at all the beautiful sweets to eat, and at that moment I thought nothing could be better. To my disappointment, my uncle asked for the house special and shooed him away. A few minutes later the server rolled out another cart with a silver dome. He lifted the dome to reveal a cake that looked like it had been made from clouds. He poured a liquid over it, then ignited the clouds into a big fireball. The first bite was a combination of hot and cold at the same time: to my amazement, it was filled luxuriously with ice cream. Anytime I see a flaming dessert now brings me back to that evening, and as an adult I still can't resist delighting in this kind of magic. Surprise your guests with this decadent treat!

SPECIAL EQUIPMENT: *3-quart metal bowl, pastry brush, culinary torch*

FOR THE ICE CREAM CAKE

Vegetable oil for brushing

1 cup brandy, plus more for igniting if you like

1 cup dried cherries

½ teaspoon ground cinnamon

4 ounces dark chocolate, roughly chopped

1½ quarts vanilla ice cream, softened

¼ cup water

2 tablespoons unsalted butter, melted

2 tablespoons sugar

One 9-inch store-bought pound cake

FOR THE MERINGUE

1 cup egg whites (from about 6 large eggs), at room temperature

Pinch of cream of tartar

1 cup sugar

To make the ice cream cake: Fashion a 3-quart metal bowl into a cake mold by brushing it with vegetable oil. Line the inside with plastic wrap and leave a 1-inch overhang around the edges.

In a small saucepan, combine ¾ cup of the brandy with the dried cherries. Bring to a simmer over medium heat and simmer for 5 minutes. Strain the brandy into a bowl and reserve the cherries; allow both to cool.

Gently stir the dried cherries, cinnamon, and dark chocolate pieces to the softened ice cream until just combined.

In a small bowl, whisk together the water, butter, sugar, and the remaining ¼ cup brandy. Cut the pound cake into 1-inch-thick slices, and using a pastry brush, brush each slice with the buttered brandy mixture. With a spatula, spread half of the ice cream mixture into the bottom of the prepared bowl, evenly smoothing the surface. Next, place the pound cake slices on top of the ice cream layer, trimming pieces as needed. Top the pound cake with the rest of the ice cream, evenly smoothing the surface with the spatula again. Finish by gently pressing the remaining pound cake slices on top of the ice cream. Cover with plastic wrap and freeze for 1 hour, or until set.

To make the meringue: In a large bowl, beat the egg whites with the cream of tartar using a hand mixer on medium-high speed for about 2 minutes, until foamy. Then, on high speed, slowly beat in the sugar until the egg whites form glossy, stiff peaks.

To assemble: Remove the plastic wrap from the top of the ice cream cake bowl and carefully invert the cake onto a parchment-lined baking sheet. Remove the remaining plastic wrap and, using a spatula, cover the surface of the cake with meringue, creating a dome-shaped top. Using the back of a spoon, form swirly peaks in the meringue. Freeze the cake for another hour.

Immediately before serving, remove the cake from the freezer and use a culinary torch to brown the cake to caramelize it. (Alternatively, bake in a preheated 500°F oven until the meringue begins to turn golden, 3 to 4 minutes.) For extra theatrics, heat ½ cup brandy in a saucepan, ignite it with a long kitchen match, and pour the flaming alcohol over the cake.

TAPPING MAPLE TREES

꘎

The maple syrup that pours so easily over pancakes and into porridge is made not without hard work and a lot of patience. I'd been curious about the process and wanted to tap some trees myself, so I grabbed a friend and we adventured up to Mapleland Farms in Salem, New York.

Things were quiet on the farm. The onset of spring was palpable, but a bit of melancholy still lingered from winter's frost. Save for the sweet syrup inside, the maple trees were bare and scattered throughout the plantation in no uniform fashion. We spent the day following the farmers around, peeking into buckets, nosing around the caldrons of bubbling syrup, and snacking on maple cotton candy.

The groundsman who guided us around the farm showed us the traditional way to harvest maple syrup—manually. Three or four holes are bored into each tree, and from these punctures hang buckets that have been used to collect maple for decades. Once the buckets are full they're taken to the sugarhouse, where the sap is boiled down and filtered before it is bottled.

Back in the studio, I rekindled the memories from our trip to the farm. I thought of the crisp air upstate and entering the warm sugar shack with its sweet aromas wafting through the air. In my kitchen I opened a bottle of the syrup, dipped my finger in, and tasted its rich caramelized flavors. I imagined drizzling it over a big stack of pancakes, but also how it might give a layer of complexity to savory winter dishes.

I invited friends over for a cozy winter meal that would center around a maple-based main dish. A big pot of braised stew has always been a favorite dish of mine, and it can be made ahead of time and set aside to let its flavors deepen. As I ladled out hearty portions of braised stew onto my guests' plates, I had the chance to retell my story about all that I had learned from my maple tapping trip.

Shaved Brussels Sprout Salad *with* Cranberries *and* Almonds

Serves 6 to 8

What is it about Brussels sprouts that makes them the vegetable that kids (and adults) always complain about eating? For me it wasn't until I began preparing Brussels sprouts myself—shaving them raw and roasting them—that I came to love them. Now whenever I see these mini cabbages at the market, I grab a couple stalks to add a healthy helping of greens during the colder season months.

The bright flavors used in preparing the Brussels sprouts in this recipe will open up the minds of the cynics: the zing of the orange and the sweetness of the honey in the dressing temper any bitterness, while the cranberries and almonds add textural layers. This salad makes for a fine starter to a cozy meal; add a protein for substance and it's fit to serve as a light dinner or lunch.

2 pounds Brussels sprouts

¼ cup extra virgin olive oil

Finely grated zest and juice of 1 orange

2 tablespoons honey

⅓ cup red wine vinegar

Salt and freshly ground black pepper

¼ cup dried cranberries

¼ cup slivered toasted almonds

Using a mandoline set at ⅛ inch, shave the Brussels sprouts horizontally. Place them in a large bowl.

In a small bowl, whisk together the olive oil, orange zest and juice, honey, and vinegar. Season with salt and pepper. Gently toss the Brussels sprouts with dressing and allow to sit for at least 5 minutes to marinate in the dressing. Mix in the cranberries and toasted almonds and serve.

Maple Braised Beef Stew

Serves 6 to 8

There's nothing like the smell of the house when a beef stew has been simmering for hours. It's a slow-cooking dish that develops layers of flavor over time. I've often used beer in my marinades to tenderize the meat and found that adding sweet maple syrup provides a nice contrast to the bitterness of the ale. When it's finished braising, the meat should be falling off the bone.

Make this dish when it is extra cold outside or when the rain won't give up. By preparing the stew a few days in advice, the flavors meld together and become strong and piquant. Make a big pot for hungry dinner guests, or keep it for yourself and you'll have a comforting dish you can reheat and enjoy all week.

6 pounds bone-in short ribs

FOR THE MARINADE

4 garlic cloves, finely minced

1 tablespoon salt

2 teaspoons freshly ground black pepper

½ tablespoon fennel seeds

½ tablespoon red chile flakes

4 sprigs fresh thyme

3 sprigs fresh rosemary

¼ cup maple syrup

FOR THE STEW

2 tablespoons all-purpose flour

3 tablespoons extra virgin olive oil

3 carrots, finely chopped

3 stalks celery, finely chopped

1 cup pearl onions, peeled

2 bay leaves

2 cups porter ale

2 cups beef stock

Salt and freshly ground black pepper

In a small bowl mix together the garlic, salt, pepper, fennel, chile flakes, thyme, rosemary, and maple syrup to make a marinade. Place the ribs in a large bowl, rub the marinade over the ribs, and cover with plastic wrap. Place in the refrigerator for at least 6 hours or overnight.

Preheat the oven to 325°F.

Remove the ribs from refrigerator and bring them to room temperature. Coat each rib lightly with flour and set aside. Heat the olive oil in a large saucepan or Dutch oven over medium-high heat until hot but not smoking. Add the ribs and brown them on all sides, about 4 minutes per side. Transfer the meat to a large plate and set aside. In the same pot, add the carrots, celery, and pearl onions, reduce the heat to medium-low and sauté until the vegetables soften, about 10 minutes. Stir in the bay leaves, ale, and stock, then the ribs, and bring to a boil over medium-high heat. Remove from the heat, cover the pot, and transfer it to the oven. Braise until the meat is very tender, about 3 hours. Allow the stew to cool to room temperature, then cover and refrigerate. We like to make the stew 1 to 2 days ahead of time to let the flavors develop.

To serve, remove the stew from the refrigerator, skim the fat from the surface, and remove the bay leaves. Reheat on the stovetop over medium-low heat and season with salt and pepper. I like to serve my stew it with Celery Root, Potato, and Pear Mash (recipes follows).

Celery Root, Potato, *and* Pear Mash

Serves 6 to 8

Mashed potatoes is a standby comfort dish known for its hearty texture and simplicity. Taking note of the classic mashed potato formula, I added celery root, also called celeriac, to the recipe, and sweet pears to lighten up the dish. It's something a little different, with complex earthy flavors and a silkier texture than straight mashed potatoes.

> 3 large russet potatoes, peeled and cubed
>
> 1 medium celery root, tough outer parts removed, peeled, and cubed
>
> Salt
>
> 4 ripe pears, peeled, cored, and cut into cubes
>
> 1 cup heavy cream
>
> ½ cup (1 stick) unsalted butter, cut into cubes
>
> Freshly ground black pepper

Place the potatoes and celery root in a large saucepan and and fill with enough water to cover the vegetables by 2 inches; season generously with salt. Bring the water to a boil over medium-high heat, then reduce the heat to medium and cook until the vegetables are tender, about 25 minutes. Add the pears during the last 5 minutes of cooking. Drain and transfer to a large bowl. Mash the celery root, potatoes, and pears with a hand masher, slowly adding the heavy cream and butter to the mixture and continue to mash until well combined. Season with salt and pepper and serve.

Pecan Pie *with*
Salted Maple Ice Cream

Serves 6 to 8

Pecan pie, a southern standby, holds a special place in my heart. My college room-mate relied on baking these pies for professors to account for any lateness on school assignments. Presented along with her charming southern drawl, I'm convinced that they boosted her standing by an entire letter grade. All of the day's worries would melt away after taking a bite of her dense nutty pie set in its brown sugar filling, the flavors filling me with visions of her grandma's old-fashioned home cooking and pies cooling on racks in a country kitchen.

This pie, inspired by that roommate's, is unapologetically rich—it uses three different kinds of sugar, almost two sticks of butter, and a load of pecans. My favorite way to serve any warm pie is à la mode, with a generous scoop of ice cream on top. Here I made a batch of ice cream from the maple syrup I brought back from my farm visit; this, plus the addition of a bit of salt to the mix, creates a flavor reminiscent of salted caramel. The result is well worth the indulgence. Just try to stop yourself from eating the whole pie in one sitting.

SPECIAL EQUIPMENT: *Ceramic pie weights or dried beans for prebaking*

FOR THE DOUGH

1 cup all-purpose flour, plus more for dusting

Pinch of salt

2 tablespoons sugar

½ cup (1 stick) cold unsalted butter, cut into small chunks

¼ cup cold water

FOR THE FILLING

3 large eggs

½ cup light corn syrup

½ cup packed light brown sugar

½ cup granulated sugar

6 tablespoons unsalted butter, melted

I teaspoon vanilla extract

½ teaspoon salt

2 cups pecan halves

I teaspoon water

To make the dough: Combine the flour, salt, sugar, and butter in a food processor. Pulse for about 10 seconds, until you have pea-size pieces. Add the cold water and pulse for 2 seconds, just enough to incorporate the water into the flour. Alternatively, combine the ingredients in a bowl and mix with a pastry blender until just combined.

Transfer the dough to a work surface lightly dusted with flour and knead the dough just enough for it to come together. Form the dough into a disk, wrap with plastic, and refrigerate for at least 1 hour or up to 2 days. On the lightly floured work surface, roll the dough into a 12-inch round. Transfer the dough into a pie pan, trimming to a 1-inch overhang. Fold the extra dough over to form a rim and crimp the rim with your fingers or the underside of a fork. Prick the dough a few times with a fork. Cover with plastic wrap and freeze for 30 minutes.

Preheat the oven to 400°F.

Remove the pie pan from the freezer. Line the dough with parchment paper and fill with ceramic pie weights or dried beans. Prebake for 10 to 15 minutes, until edges begin to turn golden. Take the piecrust out of the oven and remove parchment paper and weights; lower the oven temperature to 350°F.

Meanwhile, in a large bowl, combine 2 of the eggs, the corn syrup, sugars, butter, vanilla, and salt and whisk until smooth. Gently mix in the pecans. Pour the pecan filling into the piecrust.

In a small bowl, beat the remaining egg with the water to create an egg wash and brush the edges of the pie with the egg wash. Bake the pie until the center feels set but is still soft and the pecans are deep brown in color, 40 to 50 minutes. Place the pie on a wire rack to cool. Serve slightly warm, with each slice topped with a scoop of Salted Maple Ice Cream (*recipe follows*).

SALTED MAPLE ICE CREAM (*Makes about 1 quart*)

3 cups heavy cream

¼ cup sugar

½ cup maple syrup

1 teaspoon salt

1 teaspoon vanilla extract

4 large egg yolks

In a medium saucepan, combine the heavy cream, sugar, maple syrup, and salt. Bring to a simmer over medium heat.

Meanwhile, in a medium heatproof bowl, whisk the egg yolks and vanilla. In a slow stream, gradually add the hot cream mixture to the eggs, whisking constantly to thicken the mixture without clumping. Once well combined, transfer the custard back to the saucepan and, still whisking constantly, cook over medium-low heat until mixture is thick enough to coat the back of a spoon.

Strain the custard though a sieve into a heatproof container and let it cool, then cover and refrigerate until cold, at least 4 hours or overnight. Pour into an ice cream maker and churn according to the manufacturer's instructions. Transfer the ice cream to an airtight container and freeze until firm, 3 to 4 hours.

SPRING

Nothing is so beautiful as spring—

When weeds, in wheels, shoot long and lovely and lush;

Thrush's eggs look little low heavens, and thrush

Through the echoing timber does so rinse and wring

The ear, it strikes like lightnings to hear him sing.

GERARD MANLEY HOPKINS

IN THE GARDEN

⤝⤞

*W*ith my studio in the middle of busy Manhattan, I've always wanted to come home to a neighborhood that is lined with trees and plants. A couple years ago I fell in love with Brooklyn Heights and moved to the historic neighborhood with its cobblestone streets and inspiring architectural details. I have a plot in a community garden a couple blocks from where I live, where full days are spent with my knees in the dirt and my back in the sun. Herbs drink up the sunlight in the springtime and grow up and wide. The vegetables pop up sweet and ripe straight from the earth. Radishes are ready for butter and salt, potatoes grow small and full of starch, and green beans dangle like springtime icicles. All I need for lunch is a basket and one fell swoop through the garden.

Revisiting the row of radishes I put to seed months prior is one of the most rewarding times of spring. The greens bloom and perch above while the spicy bulbs grow below: Red King, French Breakfast, Cherry Belle, Champion, and daikon radishes are all there. With a small shovel I coax the radishes from the soil, dirt still clinging to the wrinkles in their flesh and where the stems meet the roots.

After shaking the radishes free of dirt, I put them to the side and visit patches of rosemary, mint, and basil. The herb patch grows steadily, and it's time to trim their leaves. Picking sprigs of mint and basil, I daydream of throwing them into lemonade, aioli, butter, and tarts. Beside the herbs I find a narrow line of green stalks that stick up straight as a ruler from the ground; spring onions are delightful this time of year and lend acidity and brightness to omelets, bean salads, and soups. I pick green beans next; craning my neck, I peer into the webbing of the small bushes and pluck the long hanging beans from their leaves. They, too, are added to the pile of vegetables.

By the end of the day in my garden, I have enough bounty to fill my fridge and to jazz up my meals for the week. Here is a collection of dishes inspired by this awakening of spring.

Herbal Lemonade

Serves 4

Lemonade is inherently refreshing, so it's hard to imagine it could get any better. That's what I thought, until on a whim I decided to throw a handful of herbs from the garden into my glass. The combination of citrus and herbs is astounding, adding depth and bright flavors to a classic beverage. Experiment with whatever herb is overflowing in your garden or farmers' market. To transform this lemonade into a sophisticated cocktail, feel free to spike it with your favorite spirits.

    1 cup sugar

    4 cups water

    1 bunch mixed fresh herbs (I like mint, basil, and rosemary),
        plus more for garnish

    1 cup fresh lemon juice (from 5 to 6 lemons)

    1 lemon, sliced into rounds

Combine the sugar, 1 cup of the water, and the herbs in a small saucepan. Place over medium heat, bring to a simmer, and simmer, stirring until the sugar has dissolved. Set aside to cool and let the herbs steep for 15 minutes. Strain the herbal simple syrup into a jar and discard the herbs. The herbal simple syrup can be stored in the refrigerator for up to 2 weeks.

Fill a large pitcher with ice and pour in the remaining 3 cups water with the lemon juice. Start by adding ½ cup herbal simple syrup, taste, and add more if you like, until it's sweet enough for your taste. Finish with the lemon slices and sprigs of fresh herbs.

Radishes *with* Citrus Tarragon Butter

Serves 4

When visiting France, my favorite afternoon snack is radishes from the market with fresh-churned butter and chunky sea salt. I decided to update the classic pairing and throw tarragon into the mix to add a quick layer of extra flavor. The result is bright and tangy with an anise-like finish that offsets the spice of the radishes. The secret to making this dish sing is using the freshest radishes you can find. French radishes are my top choice; they should be fire engine red with white tips and a crunchy texture. To make a perfect bite, smear butter generously onto a radish and sprinkle with flakes of sea salt. For a heartier snack, pair the buttered radishes with a fresh baguette—so simple and so delicious.

> ½ cup (1 stick) unsalted butter, softened
>
> 2 tablespoons chopped fresh tarragon
>
> 1 tablespoon fresh lemon juice
>
> Zest of 1 lemon
>
> Salt and freshly ground black pepper
>
> 1 bunch mixed radishes, trimmed and cut in half
>
> Flaky sea salt (I like Maldon or fleur de sel)

In a small bowl, combine the butter, tarragon, lemon juice, zest, and a pinch of salt and pepper; stir with a spoon to incorporate the ingredients. Transfer the butter mixture to a ramekin and keep at room temperature to serve. Enjoy the radishes with a generous spread of citrus tarragon butter and sprinkling of flaky sea salt. Store leftover butter covered in plastic wrap in the refrigerator for up to 1 week. Bring back to room temperature before serving again.

Note: Herbed butter can be used as a last-minute flavor boost to pasta dishes, steamed vegetables, or grilled fish or meat dishes.

Asparagus *and* Spring Onion Tart

Serves 4

Whenever I crave a little something decadent for lunch, a vegetable tart is my fall-back dish—rich but somehow still light. Asparagus is one of the first vegetables to pop up all over the farmers' markets during the start of spring, and with its spear-like shape, feathery tips, and distinctive flavor, set atop a generous sprinkling of cheese it makes the perfect topping for the simple base of a buttery, flaky pastry.

I sheet thawed store-bought puff pastry dough

I large egg, beaten with I teaspoon water

½ cup grated Gruyère or Comté cheese

½ cup Fontina cheese

8 ounces asparagus, trimmed

8 ounces spring onions, trimmed and cut in half lengthwise

Extra virgin olive oil for brushing

Salt and freshly ground black pepper

Edible flower blossoms (optional)

Roll out the thawed puff pastry dough to about ⅛ inch thick on a lightly floured surface and cut it into an approximately 10 x 8-inch rectangle. Place the dough on a baking sheet lined with parchment paper. Using a paring knife, score a border ½ inch in from the edge of the dough and brush the border with the egg wash. Using a fork, prick all over through the center of the dough. Transfer to the refrigerator and chill for at least 15 minutes.

Preheat the oven to 400°F.

Parbake the pastry dough for 8 to 10 minutes, until the pastry begins to puff up, using a fork to prick any air pockets. Scatter the cheeses evenly over the center of the pastry dough, keeping the border clean. Arrange the asparagus spears and green onions to fit closely together on the pastry, alternating between the two. Drizzle with olive oil and season with salt and pepper. Brush the edges of the dough with egg wash again and bake until the crust is golden and the vegetables are cooked through, about 20 minutes. The tart can be served warm or at room temperature. Finish with a scattering of edible flower blossoms if desired.

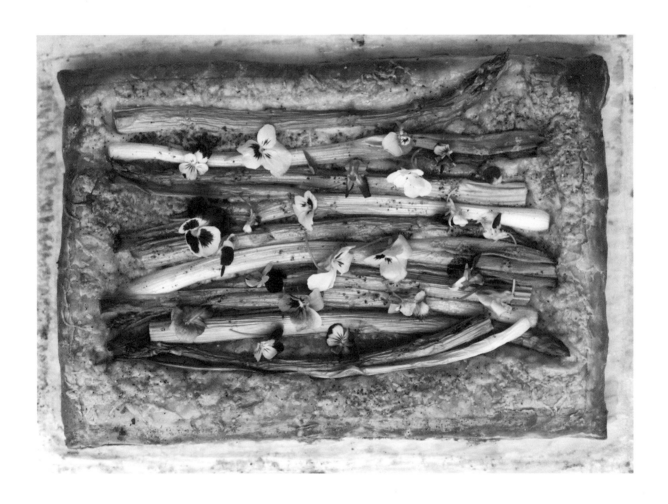

Poached Salmon Salad *with* Garden Vegetables

Serves 4

Poaching is the gentlest form of cooking and is perfect for delicate proteins like fish that you don't want to overcook. Simmering the salmon over a low heat allows it to keep a beautiful, slightly translucent center, and adding wine and fresh herbs to the poaching liquid gives the salmon a fragrant finish. Paired with spring vegetables, this dish is brightly subtle and perfectly fresh.

FOR THE SALMON

½ cup dry white wine, such as Sauvignon Blanc

2 tablespoons Pernod

½ teaspoon salt

2 sprigs dill

1 shallot, cut in half and sliced

8 ounces salmon boneless, skinless salmon fillet

1 bunch watercress, root ends trimmed

1 cup sugar snap peas, strings removed and cut into thin strips

½ cup fresh or frozen English peas, cooked

½ pound baby heirloom tomatoes, halved

To make the salmon: In a medium skillet, combine the wine, Pernod, salt, dill sprigs, and shallot. Add the salmon along with enough water to cover the fish and bring to a simmer over medium heat. Cook until the salmon is opaque, 5 to 7 minutes. We prefer to undercook ours slightly so the fish remains tender. Transfer the salmon to a dish, let cool, and cover with plastic wrap. Place in the freezer until chilled, about 5 minutes. The salmon can be prepared ahead of time and kept covered in the refrigerator for up to 1 day. Once chilled, break the salmon into large pieces with a fork and set aside.

On a large platter, arrange the watercress into a bed and top with the salmon, sugar snap peas, English peas, and tomatoes. Drizzle with the dressing (*recipe follows*) and serve immediately.

FOR THE DRESSING
1 teaspoon Dijon mustard
1 garlic clove, finely chopped
¼ cup champagne vinegar
1 tablespoon chopped fresh dill
½ cup extra virgin olive oil
Salt and freshly ground black pepper

To make the dressing: In a small bowl, whisk together the mustard, garlic, vinegar, and chopped dill. Continue to whisk while adding the olive oil in a slow, steady stream until the dressing is emulsified. Season with salt and pepper.

Gingered Rhubarb *and* Mascarpone Parfait

Serves 4

In the early spring, rhubarb is a hot commodity at the farmers' market—its season is brief and it's a sign of warmer weather to come. Crisp and tart, rhubarb awakens the taste buds that winter held hostage and lends itself perfectly to spring and summer appetites.

Rhubarb is commonly simmered with sugar and made into a filling for pie, but here we were thinking outside the crust and decided upon a parfait instead. Married with lemon, the rhubarb's tart edge is brightened, creating a beautifully flavored and pink-kissed compote. This compote would be equally lovely served alongside a selection of local cheeses, stewed into a sauce, or served with a scoop of ice cream.

I pound rhubarb, peeled and cut into ½-inch pieces

2 cups Gewürztraminer or sweet Riesling wine

I cup granulated sugar

One 3-inch piece ginger, sliced

Peel of I lemon

I cup mascarpone cheese, at room temperature

I tablespoon confectioners' sugar

Grated zest and juice of I orange

I vanilla bean, split and seeds scraped

I cup granola (I like Nature's Path granola)

2 tablespoons pistachios, toasted and chopped

Preheat the oven to 400°F.

Place the rhubarb, wine, granulated sugar, ginger, and lemon peel in a 9 x 13-inch baking dish and gently toss to combine. Place in the oven and bake for 45 minutes. Remove from oven and set aside.

In a medium bowl, combine the mascarpone, confectioners' sugar, orange zest and juice, and the seeds from the vanilla bean and stir until well combined.

Create 4 parfaits by layering the ingredients in glasses in the following order: rhubarb compote, mascarpone cream, and granola. Garnish with pistachios and serve.

BREAKFAST IN BED

⇥⇤

*O*ne *of my greatest pleasures* while traveling is ordering room service for breakfast. When I hear the knock at my door, I perk up and nearly lose the towel coiled atop my head. In my bathrobe, I scurry to answer the call of my breakfast. I order the works—a big glass of freshly squeezed OJ, coffee, poached eggs on toast, bacon, and a side of fruit. I roll the table bedside and climb back into bed with my favorite book and damp hair, taking my time to eat and allowing myself the luxury of a morning in the sheets.

Travel shouldn't be the only excuse to indulge in a simple meal bedside. Once the weekend rolls around, we can keep our e-mails at bay and leave our pajamas on a little longer. It's good to break the rules sometimes and take pleasure in eating in bed. Take the time to sip your coffee a little slower and enjoy reading the paper while basking in the morning sun.

The following are ideas and inspiration to create an at-home version of breakfast in bed, perfect for lazy weekends around the house. Add some spice to your coffee, some flame to your grapefruit, and a little tang to your eggs. Whether you are enjoying breakfast by yourself or treating someone else, these recipes will give you a little taste of vacation without having to leave your home.

Cardamom Coffee

Adding spices and a pinch of salt to my morning coffee pot is a habit I developed after drinking a delicious spiced Turkish coffee that accompanied a flaky baklava dessert. This recipe makes a delicious cup of joe to enjoy in the early hours, but it also serves as a lovely sip after dinner. I chose to use cardamom for its aroma and its slight smokiness, but you can play around with any spice that inspires you. Ground cinnamon, cloves, nutmeg, and star anise would also be wonderful.

SPECIAL EQUIPMENT: *Stovetop espresso coffee maker or French press*

Ground coffee beans

1 cardamom pod per cup of coffee, cracked

Salt

Milk and sugar

In an espresso coffee maker or French press, brew your coffee as usual, adding a cracked cardamom pod and pinch of salt per cup to the ground coffee before brewing. Add milk and sugar to your liking. The end result should be smooth with a floral spiced aroma.

Minted Grapefruit Brûlée

Serves 2

Adding a crunchy layer of brûléed sugar to the top of your grapefruit transforms an everyday fruit into something special. When you've eaten your way to the rind, there will be a puddle of grapefruit juice lingering at the bottom; be sure to drink up this delicious nectar.

1 grapefruit, cut in half crosswise

2 tablespoons raw turbinado sugar

1 tablespoon chopped toasted walnuts

1 tablespoon chopped fresh mint

Preheat the broiler.

With a sharp knife, cut a thin slice off the bottoms of the grapefruit halves (just the rind) to create a flat surface. With a paper towel, gently blot the cut sides of grapefruit halves to remove any excess liquid. Set the grapefruit halves on a baking sheet and sprinkle the sugar evenly over each half. Place under the broiler and broil for 5 minutes, or until golden brown. Alternatively, you can use a culinary torch to heat the sugar until it is melted and begins to bubble and turn amber in color.

Finish each grapefruit half with a scattering of walnuts and mint and serve.

Turkish-Style Eggs *with* Yogurt

Serves 2

Sumac trees produce small fruits called drupes, and these fruits are ground into a fine powder to make the spice with the same name. Sumac is incredibly versatile and can be used to add a hint of lemony flavor to anything from eggs to hummus, making it a fantastic addition to your spice reserve. In this recipe it adds a tart, fruity finish to the eggs.

2 tablespoons extra virgin olive oil

1 cup Greek yogurt

1 garlic clove, finely minced

Squeeze of fresh lemon juice

1 teaspoon ground sumac (finely grated lemon zest can be substituted)

Salt and freshly ground black pepper

2 tablespoons unsalted butter

4 fresh sage leaves, torn

1 teaspoon white distilled vinegar

2 large eggs

Warmed pita bread or toast for dipping

In a small bowl, combine the olive oil, yogurt, garlic, lemon juice, and sumac. Season with salt and pepper. Divide the yogurt mixture between 2 small ramekins.

In a small saucepan, melt the butter over medium heat and add a pinch of salt.

Add the sage and fry until the butter becomes golden brown, about 30 seconds. Remove from the heat and set aside. Strain butter and reserve leaves.

In a large saucepan, bring about 3 inches of water to a rolling boil over high heat. Reduce the heat to a simmer and add the vinegar. Crack 1 egg into a small cup and gently slip it into the water bath, taking care that you don't break the yolk.

When the egg white has cooked through but the yolk is still runny, 3 to 4 minutes, gently remove it with a slotted spoon and transfer to a paper towel–lined plate. Repeat with the second egg.

Add a poached egg to each of the ramekins and finish each with a drizzling of the sage butter and another sprinkling of salt. Top with crispy sage leaves. Serve with warmed pita or toast for dipping and sopping up the yolk and sauce.

Goat Cheese Pancakes *with* Blackberry Compote

Serves 2 to 4; makes 6 to 8 pancakes

Sitting down to a big stack of pancakes for a weekend breakfast at home always makes me giddy. I break out the cast-iron griddle, which is my secret to pancakes with perfect crisp edges and fluffy melt-in-your-mouth centers.

In this recipe, goat cheese is folded into the batter to add a layer of richness and moistness to the pancakes.

FOR THE BLACKBERRY COMPOTE

½ cup water

¼ cup sugar

1½ cups fresh or frozen blackberries

1 tablespoon fresh lemon juice

Pinch of ground cinnamon

FOR THE PANCAKES

4 ounces soft goat cheese, crumbled

1 large egg, beaten

1 cup milk

2 tablespoons unsalted butter, melted

½ teaspoon vanilla extract

2 tablespoons sugar

2 teaspoons baking powder

Pinch of salt

Finely grated zest of 1 lemon

1 cup all-purpose flour

To make the Blackberry Compote: In a medium saucepan, combine the water, sugar, blackberries, lemon juice, and cinnamon. Place over medium heat and bring to a

boil, then lower the heat and simmer, stirring constantly until the mixture thickens and blackberries begin to soften, about 10 minutes. Cover and set aside to keep warm.

To make the pancakes: preheat the oven to 200°F.

In a large bowl, combine the goat cheese, egg, milk, butter, and vanilla, and using an electric mixer on medium speed, beat until just combined. Reduce the speed to low and add the sugar, baking powder, salt, and lemon zest. Slowly add the flour until just mixed—lumps are okay—you want to keep the batter as light and airy as possible.

Oil a large cast-iron skillet or griddle and heat it thoroughly over medium heat. Spoon ¼ cup batter onto the skillet for each pancake (making 2 or 3 at a time depending on the size of your skillet) and cook for 1 to 2 minutes, until bubbles form on the surface and the underside is lightly browned. Flip over and cook the other side until golden. Repeat until all the batter is used up. Keep the pancakes warm in the oven until you are ready to eat. Serve in stacks with the warm Blackberry Compote.

TEA PARTY

⤢

The sound of birds fluttering and chirping begins outside my window and flowers blossom on the trees in my neighborhood. Spring has awakened the world outside and we begin to feel social again after a cold winter of keeping to ourselves indoors. It's time to invite some of my favorite people over for a leisurely afternoon of tea, food, and crafting.

The basic concept of a tea party is everything I love in a small gathering: a room filled with my closest girlfriends, snacks that are small and thoughtful, and an excuse to use the pretty antique teacups I've collected over the years from flea markets that otherwise remain on their shelves.

My girlfriends and I share a love of making things by hand. Whether it's knitting a scarf for someone we love, cutting and folding paper crafts, gluing this or taking an X-Acto knife to that, the process is rewarding, and doing it together scratches the itch for socializing at the same time. Nothing is more perfect to pair with teatime.

Before anyone arrives, I set the dining room table with skeins of yarn, wooden crochet sticks and knitting needles, card stock, glue sticks, paints and scissors, and whatever else I find in my stash of craft materials. I welcome my friends to bring over their creative projects and an appetite.

A kettle of water warms over a flame while I pull down teacups and saucers from high in my cupboard. The china is delicate and thin. Some have a spiral of flowers painted around the rim, others are blue like robin eggs. I fill small bowls with loose teas and lay a stack of empty tea bags beside the twigs and leaves. Scones, still warm from the oven, are placed on platters and I line up little quiches on a tray. The kettle whistles and I hear the first knock on the door—the tea party begins.

Homemade Tea Mixtures

Boxes and tins of prepacked tea aren't your only option for a tea party. For fun you can let the ladies make their own tea combinations, laying out bowls of single herbs with little spoons and empty tea bags with milk and honey alongside, then let the party unfold. Or you can simply make your own blends. The herb mixtures listed here are a great place to start, but feel free to experiment with whatever tastes and smells strike your fancy—chamomile flowers, licorice root, dried orange peel—the options are many. Hand-blended tea mixtures also make lovely gifts. Combine your herbs in a glass jar or tin, write a simple label, and add ribbon or twine to dress it up.

FLORAL HERBAL TISANE (*Makes about 1 cup dried tea mixture, for about 16 cups of tea*)

1 tablespoon dried lavender blossoms

¾ cup dried lemon verbena

1 tablespoon dried rose petals

2 tablespoons dried mint

Mix all the ingredients together and store in a tin or jar until ready to use. Use 1 tablespoon per cup of boiling water and steep for 5 to 10 minutes. This caffeine-free tea can be enjoyed with a bit of honey and served hot or cold over ice.

SPICED BLACK TEA (*Makes about 1 cup dried tea mixture, for about 16 cups of tea*)

1 tablespoon cardamom pods, cracked

1 tablespoon ground cinnamon

2 tablespoons diced dried orange rind

¾ cup Ceylon black tea

1 teaspoon ground ginger

Mix all the ingredients together and store in a tin or jar until ready to use. Use 1 teaspoon per cup of boiling water and steep for 3 to 5 minutes. This tea goes well with a bit of milk and honey.

Black Tea Scones *with* Citrus Curd

Makes 12 scones

The scone is borderline savory and just a tiny bit sweet, perfect for slathering with generous helpings of butter and curd. As a lover of scones, I've experimented with many recipes, and this is the one I like best for a tea party. Adding ground black tea leaves to the dough gives an earthy aroma and fine crunchy texture to the scones, mirroring the flavors of the tea. A hot cup of tea made with the same variety of leaves is the perfect pairing.

2 teaspoons black tea leaves

2 cups all-purpose flour

¼ cup sugar

1 tablespoon baking powder

1 tablespoon grated orange zest

Pinch of salt

4 tablespoons (½ stick) unsalted butter, cut into cubes

¾ cup heavy cream

½ teaspoon vanilla extract

Butter for serving

Citrus Curd (recipe follows)

Place oven racks near the center of the oven and preheat to 425°F. Line 2 baking sheets with parchment paper.

Using a clean coffee grinder or mortar and pestle, grind the tea leaves into a powder. In a large bowl, combine the flour, sugar, baking powder, tea powder, orange zest, and salt. With a pastry blender or your fingers, mix the butter into the dry ingredients until the mixture becomes crumbly and coarse in texture. Add the heavy cream and vanilla and mix together with a fork until a dough begins to form. Transfer to a lightly floured work surface and knead the dough until it just comes together. Be careful not to overknead.

Divide the dough in half, forming it into two 5-inch discs about ¾ inch thick and cut each disc into 6 wedges. Transfer the scones to the prepared baking sheets, leaving 2 inches of space between them. Bake the scones until golden and a toothpick inserted into a scone comes out clean, 12 to 15 minutes. Transfer the scones to wire racks to cool. Serve warm with fresh butter and Citrus Curd (recipe follows).

CITRUS CURD

2 large eggs

2 large egg yolks

¾ cup sugar

½ cup (1 stick) unsalted butter

Finely grated zest and juice of 1 lime

⅓ cup fresh grapefruit juice

In a large bowl, whisk together the eggs, egg yolks, and sugar.

In a medium saucepan, melt the butter over low heat. Stir in the egg mixture along with the lime juice and zest and grapefruit juice. Stir continuously until thickened, 10 to 15 minutes. Pour into a jar and let cool. Cover and refrigerate until firm, at least 1 hour. The citrus curd can be made ahead of time and stored covered in the refrigerator for up to 1 week.

Mini Pea, Mint, *and* Feta Quiches

Makes twelve 4-inch tarts

These individual mini quiches are a little bit breakfast, and a little bit lunch. The creaminess of the eggs are accented by sweet peas and finished with the bright flavors of fresh mint. Feel free to make this as one large quiche if you don't have small pans on hand.

SPECIAL EQUIPMENT: *Twelve 4-inch tart pans with removable bottoms; ceramic pie weights or dried beans for prebaking*

FOR THE DOUGH

2½ cups all-purpose flour, plus more for dusting

1 teaspoon salt

1 cup (2 sticks) cold unsalted butter, cut into small chunks

½ cup cold water

FOR THE FILLING

6 large eggs

½ cup heavy cream

½ teaspoon salt

4 small unpeeled potatoes, boiled and cut into ½-inch rounds

½ cup peas

¼ cup roughly chopped fresh mint, plus more for finishing

¼ cup crumbled feta cheese

To make the dough: Place the flour, salt, and butter in a food processor. Pulse for about 10 seconds, until you have pea-size butter pieces. Sprinkle in the cold water and pulse for about 2 seconds, just enough to incorporate the water into the flour.

Transfer the dough to a lightly floured work surface and knead until it just comes together. Roll the dough into a 2-inch-diameter log, wrap with plastic, and refrigerate for at least 1 hour or up to 6 hours. Divide the dough into 12 portions. On a lightly floured surface, roll each portion into a 6-inch round. Transfer the rounds into tart pans, trim the edges with a sharp knife, and prick the dough a few times with a fork. Cover with plastic wrap and freeze for 30 minutes. (If I have room in my freezer I like to place the tart pans on baking sheets—this makes covering and moving them easier.)

Preheat the oven to 400°F.

Remove the tart pans from the freezer. Line each with parchment paper and fill them with ceramic pie weights or dried beans. Prebake for 10 minutes.

To make the filling: In a large bowl, whisk the eggs with the heavy cream and salt until smooth. Gently mix in the potato rounds, peas, and mint. Remove the tart shells from the oven and remove the weights and parchment. Set aside to cool. Lower the oven temperature to 350°F. Divide the egg filling among the tart shells and scatter the feta on top. Bake the quiches until the centers are set but are still soft, about 20 minutes. Transfer the quiches to wire racks and let cool to room temperature before removing them from the tart pans. Serve garnished with mint.

Mini Strawberry Cakes

Makes 2 dozen mini cakes

This recipe is great tea-pairing fare—the cakes look so pretty stacked on a tiered cake stand with their strawberry garnished tops—making them perfect for your next gathering of girlfriends, baby shower, bridal shower, or as a special treat for yourself.

SPECIAL EQUIPMENT: *One 24-hole mini muffin pan*

6 tablespoons unsalted butter, softened, plus extra for greasing the pan

1 cup all-purpose flour, plus extra for dusting

1 teaspoon baking powder

Pinch of salt

½ cup milk

½ teaspoon vanilla extract

1 cup confectioners' sugar, plus extra for dusting

2 large egg whites, at room temperature

24 small fresh strawberries

¼ cup cold heavy cream

½ cup strawberry jam

Preheat the oven to 350°F. Prepare a 24-hole mini muffin pan by greasing it with butter and lightly dusting it with flour.

In a large bowl, mix together the flour, baking powder, and salt. Combine the milk and vanilla in a separate bowl.

Place the butter in a large bowl; beat with an electric mixer at medium speed until pale and creamy. Gradually add the confectioners' sugar and continue to beat until light and fluffy, about 3 minutes. Reduce the mixer speed to low and add

the flour mixture in 3 additions, alternating with the milk mixture in 2 additions so you start and end with the flour. Mix until the batter comes together. Transfer to a large bowl.

In a separate large bowl, beat the egg whites with an electric mixer at medium speed until stiff peaks form. Gently fold the whites into the batter in thirds, taking care to keep it airy.

Spoon the batter into the muffin tin, filling the cups to about ½ inch from the top. Finish by pushing a strawberry into the top of each mold. Bake for 18 to 20 minutes, until a toothpick inserted in the center of the cake comes out clean. Remove from the oven and let cool completely on a wire rack, then cut the top off each cake.

In a large bowl, beat the heavy cream until it thickens into soft whipped cream. Spread each cake bottom with 1 teaspoon of strawberry jam and 1 teaspoon whipped cream. Top with the cake tops and dust lightly with confectioners' sugar.

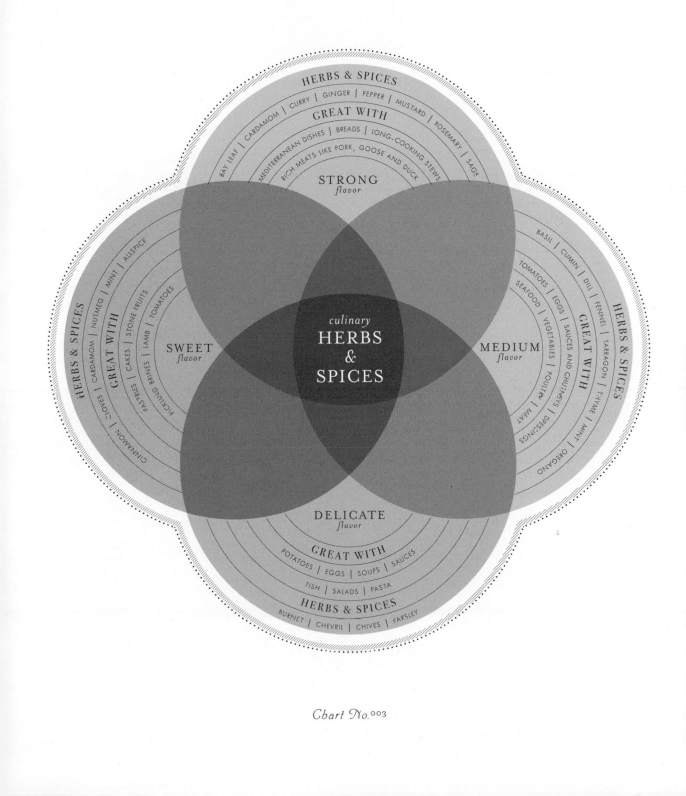

HERBS & SPICES
BAY LEAF | CARDAMOM | CURRY | GINGER | PEPPER | MUSTARD | ROSEMARY | SAGE
GREAT WITH
MEDITERRANEAN DISHES | BREADS | LONG-COOKING STEWS
RICH MEATS LIKE PORK, GOOSE AND DUCK
STRONG
flavor

HERBS & SPICES
CINNAMON | CLOVES | CARDAMOM | NUTMEG | MINT | ALLSPICE
GREAT WITH
PICKLING BRINES | PASTRIES | CAKES | STONE FRUITS | LAMB | TOMATOES
SWEET
flavor

culinary
HERBS & SPICES

MEDIUM
flavor
HERBS & SPICES
BASIL | CUMIN | DILL | FENNEL | TARRAGON | THYME | MINT | OREGANO
GREAT WITH
TOMATOES | EGGS | SAUCES AND CHUTNEYS | DRESSINGS
SEAFOOD | VEGETABLES | POULTRY | MEAT

DELICATE
flavor
GREAT WITH
POTATOES | EGGS | SOUPS | SAUCES
FISH | SALADS | PASTA
HERBS & SPICES
BURNET | CHEVRIL | CHIVES | PARSLEY

Chart No. 003

DATE NIGHT

⤨

I am always behind the stove in the studio. By the time I get home at the end of the day, the cook has been cooked out of me. But when it comes to making a meal for someone special—whether it's your boyfriend, husband, or a new certain some-one—it's easy to rally. Enjoying a meal together in the comfort of my home allows me to linger at the table all evening and truly settle into each other's company. I take time to set the table with a pair of my favorite Laguiole steak knives, forks, plates, and long tapered candles to set off a warm glow in the room. Then I step into the kitchen, tie on a crisp apron, and set to work preparing a meal, cooking my affections into each bite.

I've built this dinner menu around simple but classic steak. There is a huge amount of satisfaction in cutting through a steak and seeing an even-colored rare interior all the way through. Any guy knows he's in for a special treat when he sees a big juicy steak being plated up.

I keep the rest of the menu simple and easy—it allows me to relax and hang around in the kitchen together while dinner is cooking away. I can pull a set of wine glasses off the shelves, open up the nice bottle of red I've been saving, and look forward to a romantic evening together.

Bibb Lettuce Salad *with* Avocados *and* Tomatoes

Serves 2

A date night meal is best started off with a salad—it cleanses the palate and warms up the appetite. In this salad tender Bibb lettuce is paired with creamy avocado and tossed with lemony yogurt dressing. It's a little bit light and a little bit decadent, just as date night should be.

If you can't find nice tomatoes, grapefruit makes a great substitute, complementing the existing flavors and giving the salad a bright finish.

I ripe avocado

3 tablespoons fresh lemon juice

$^1\!/_3$ cup extra virgin olive oil

2 tablespoons plain yogurt

2 tablespoons chopped fresh flat-leaf parsley

I garlic clove, minced

Salt and freshly ground black pepper

I small head Bibb lettuce, leaves torn

I tomato, cut into wedges

Cut the avocado in half and remove the pit and peel. In a food processor, combine half the avacado, the lemon juice, olive oil, yogurt, parsley, and garlic and process until smooth. Season with salt and pepper.

Slice the remaining avocado half. Divide the lettuce between 2 plates, top with the tomato wedges and avocado slices, and drizzle with the dressing.

Dry-Aged Steak *with* Chive Butter

Serves 2

To hit your date's sweet spot, prepare a steak. The secret to a great steak is choosing a quality piece of meat. Go your local butcher for the freshest picks and ask them for their recommendations. The best steaks come from the short loin, sirloin, and rib sections located in the middle of the cow. My favorite cut is the rib eye, which is full of flavor, finely marbled, and juicy with a nice chew. Filet mignon is known to be the most tender cut of beef if you're the type that likes your steaks to be dainty. The manliest of steaks would be the porterhouse, which is a huge steak that includes both the tenderloin and strip steak. I love the inherent smokiness present in a steak that is dry aged. For this occasion, rather than throwing the steak on a grill or in a skillet, I prepare it in a way that takes a little bit extra time and care: I turn the oven to a low temperature and let the juices circulate for nearly an hour. The end result is a juicy steak with a pink center every time. This technique is foolproof (it works wonders with lamb and duck too) and gives me time to mingle with my date as the steak bakes in the oven.

> 2 dry-aged boneless rib eye steaks (1 to 1½ pounds),
>   1 inch thick, at room temperature
> Extra virgin olive oil for brushing
> Chive Butter (recipe follows)
> Salt and freshly ground black pepper

Preheat the oven to 225°F.

Wrap each steak loosely in foil and place them on roasting rack over a baking sheet. Place in the oven and bake for 40 to 50 minutes, until the internal temperature reaches 130°F; insert a meat thermometer into the center of the thickest part of the steak to test the temperature. Remove from the oven and unwrap the

steaks from the foil. Pat the steaks dry with a paper towel and brush with olive oil. Heat a cast-iron skillet over high heat until it's hot, then sear the steaks for 20 seconds on each side—this will give them a caramelized crust while keeping them tender and juicy on the inside. Before removing the steaks from the pan, finish by adding a pat of Chive Butter. Transfer to 2 plates, let rest for 2 minutes, then season with salt and pepper and serve with more chive butter as you like.

CHIVE BUTTER
½ cup (1 stick) unsalted butter, softened
2 tablespoons chopped fresh chives
1 tablespoon fresh lemon juice
Salt and freshly ground black pepper

In a small bowl, combine the butter, chives, lemon juice, and a pinch of salt and pepper; stir with a spoon to incorporate the ingredients. Transfer the mixture to a sheet of parchment paper and form a log approximately 1½ inches in diameter. Roll the parchment tightly around the butter and twist the ends of the paper. Refrigerate for at least 2 hours for the butter to firm. Slice as needed for steaks. Any leftover butter can be stored covered in plastic wrap in the refrigerator for up to 1 week. This butter would also be delicious spread over warm fresh bread to accompany your steak dinner.

Cumin Glazed Carrots

Serves 2

Carrots are at their sweetest in the springtime. When glazed with sweet honey and sprinkled with cumin, they become so tasty you'll forego your fork and eat them with your fingers—not a bad move for a date night. This recipe is still delicious if you can't get your hands on thin spring carrots—just peel and quarter larger carrots lengthwise so they're long and slender.

    2 tablespoons extra virgin olive oil
    1 bunch long baby carrots, scrubbed, green stems trimmed to 1 inch
    1 tablespoon honey
    ½ teaspoon ground cumin
    Salt and freshly ground black pepper
    1 tablespoon fresh lemon juice
    2 tablespoons chopped fresh cilantro

Heat the olive oil in a large skillet over medium-low heat. Add the carrots, honey, and cumin. Stir and season with salt and pepper. Cover the skillet and cook for 5 minutes, stirring occasionally.

Uncover the pan and raise the heat to medium. Continue to cook, stirring occasionally, until the carrots become tender and begin to brown, 8 to 10 minutes.

Remove the pan from heat and stir in the lemon juice. Sprinkle with the cilantro and serve.

Raspberry Eton Mess

Serves 2

The end of a date night meal is as important as the beginning. For dessert I prepare a sweet that is equal parts sexy, messy, and easy. An Eton mess is a pretty, light English dessert. Two spoons, one glass, and a handful of berries—the perfect dish to share.

> ¾ cup raspberries, plus more for garnish
>
> 1 tablespoon sugar
>
> 2 teaspoons sweet Riesling or dessert wine
>
> 1 cup cold heavy cream
>
> Three 3-inch store-bought meringues, roughly crumbled

Place the raspberries into a bowl and add the sugar and wine. Crush the berries with the back of a spoon and mix to a jamlike texture. Set aside.

In a large bowl using an electric mixer, beat the heavy cream on medium-low speed until soft peaks form.

Fill a dessert glass with a layer of whipped cream, followed by a spoonful of the raspberry-wine mixture and a sprinkling of meringue pieces. Repeat until the glass is full, finishing with a final layer of whipped cream and a few whole berries.

CHILDHOOD FAVORITES

When I was a kid, no one could pry the Cherry Coke from my fingertips. Whenever my mother would allow me a soda, I savored every sip and every bubble that tickled my nose. When the bottle was dry, I would have a ring of pink cherry syrup lining the rim of my mouth. The hiss of a cola bottle when the top cracks open still sends warm waves of nostalgia spiraling through my system.

In the studio I take care to craft menus that are sophisticated and have a sense of elegance beneath the surface. Nonetheless, in the midst of all the technique and splendor of ingredients, at times I need something familiar to satisfy my appetite—I can't help but crave the flavors of my past. As an adult I rarely revisit my old favorites, but every now and then nothing will scratch that itch quite like a bowl of mac and cheese or the crunch of a handful of Cracker Jacks. For this reason, I created this selection of recipes to transport me back to days spent outdoors with grass-stained knees, games of flashlight tag, and all the fixings of a perfect meal from childhood. When I begin to feel a longing for those days, I invite a few old pals over, pull out the box of Scrabble hiding behind the bookshelf, share these nostalgic treats, and make a go of being twelve again.

Cherry Cola

Makes about 3 ½ cups cherry syrup, for 14 servings of soda

Don't underestimate the value of a homemade cola—it might be easy to pop open a store-bought bottle as we did when we were kids, but this stuff is magic. Cherry Coke is my weakness, and thus this recipe was born—it is the cola recipe that ruins all other cola recipes. If you crave a little nostalgia with your soda, consider this concoction your own.

SPECIAL EQUIPMENT: *Cheesecloth*

2 ½ cups water

Finely grated zest of 1 lemon

Finely grated zest of 2 oranges

Finely grated zest of 2 limes

Large pinch of freshly grated nutmeg

1 cinnamon stick

½ star anise pod

½ teaspoon dried lavender flowers

One 2-inch knob ginger, peeled and sliced

¼ teaspoon citric acid (found in the baking aisle of grocery stores or health food stores)

1 ½ pounds fresh cherries, stems removed, cut in half, and pitted

2 cups superfine sugar

2 tablespoons light brown sugar

Seltzer for topping

In a medium saucepan, combine the water, lemon zest, orange zest, lime zest, nutmeg, cinnamon stick, star anise, lavender, ginger, and citric acid. Tie the cherries up in cheesecloth and submerge them in the liquid. Place over medium heat and bring to a boil, then reduce the heat to low and simmer for 25 minutes, or until the cherries soften and their juices are released and the syrup is deep red in color.

In a large bowl combine the sugars. Place a fine sieve over the bowl, remove the cherries from the saucepan, and place them in the sieve. Using a wooden spoon, press any extra syrup or cherry liquid from the bundle. Reserve the cooked cherries to use as a topping for desserts. Strain the rest of syrup from saucepan through the sieve and into the bowl. Discard the spices and stir the syrup until the sugar dissolves. Cool completely, then transfer to a jar, cover, and refrigerate until ready to use. The finished syrup can be made ahead and stored in the refrigerator for up to 1 week.

To make the cherry cola: Fill a glass with ice; pour in ¼ cup cherry syrup and top with about 1 cup seltzer water, stir, and top with a fresh cherry.

Note: The cooked cherries can be stored covered in a glass jar and kept in the refrigerator for up to 1 week. They are great spooned over plain yogurt for breakfast or as an accompaniment to ice cream.

How to Halve & Pit
CHERRIES

TO HALVE AND PIT CHERRIES, first remove the stems, then using a paring knife, cut lengthwise all the way around the cherry. Using your hands, pull the halves apart with a twisting motion. With a small spoon, scoop the pit from cherry halves and discard.

Mac *and* Cheese

Serves 8

Mac and cheese needs no introduction. It is childhood in a casserole dish. As an adult, you'll find it still hits the spot when you're craving a taste of comfort. In my version, the penne pasta gives a firm, chewy bite, while the delicate panko (Japanese breadcrumbs) gives it a light buttery crust.

6 tablespoons unsalted butter, plus more for the baking dish

Salt

1 pound penne pasta

½ cup all-purpose flour

4 cups milk

2 cups grated Gruyère cheese

1 cup grated Parmesan cheese

Pinch of freshly grated nutmeg

Freshly ground black pepper

1 cup panko

Preheat the oven to 375°F. Grease a shallow 3- to 4-quart baking dish with butter.

Bring a pot of salted water to a boil and add the pasta. Cook 1 to 2 minutes less than the package instructions for al dente. Drain and set aside.

In a medium saucepan, melt the butter over medium heat. Reserve 2 tablespoons of the melted butter in a small dish. Whisk the flour and milk into the pan, and, whisking continuously, bring the mixture to a boil, then reduce the heat and simmer until thickened, about 2 minutes.

Remove the sauce from the heat and whisk in the cheeses and nutmeg; season generously with salt and pepper. Toss the pasta with the sauce, coating well, and transfer to the baking dish.

Toss the panko with the reserved butter and scatter over the pasta. Transfer to the oven and bake until the top is browned and the sauce is bubbling, 20 to 25 minutes. Let cool for a few minutes before serving.

Fried Hominy *with* Chile *and* Lime

Serves 8 to 10

Hominy is a type of corn or maize that has been soaked in a lye or lime solution to soften its tough exterior. It resembles a gigantic corn kernel and puffs up deliciously when fried. Our homemade version is finished with a blend of spices and lime zest that gives a zing to your taste buds. Mexican-style hominy can be found in the Latin section of most grocery stores.

Consider these your excuse to eat corn nuts again. Only this time there are no adults around to tell you not to break a tooth.

One 29-ounce can hominy
2 teaspoons smoked paprika
1 teaspoon ground cumin
1 teaspoon Mexican chile powder (New Mexico, ancho, or chipotle)
Canola oil for frying
Grated lime zest
Salt

Preheat the oven to 275°F.

Rinse and drain the hominy, then dry it with paper towels and lay it out in a single layer on a baking sheet. Transfer it to the oven and bake for 25 to 30 minutes, until the hominy is dry.

Meanwhile, mix the spices together in a small bowl and set aside.

Heat several inches of oil in a large saucepan until it begins to shimmer or the temperature reaches 375°F on a deep-fry or candy thermometer. Fry the dried hominy in small batches without overcrowding, until crisp and brown, 4 to 5 minutes. Remove with a slotted spoon and drain on a paper towel–lined plate. Transfer to a bowl and finish by tossing with the spice mixture, lime zest, and salt if needed.

Homemade Cracker Jacks

Serves 4 to 6

I love anything with a secret prize hidden in it. As a little girl, looking forward to the reward at the bottom of my bag of cereal or box of Cracker Jacks was enough to make sure I polished off the whole thing. This recipe is inspired by the original, only better because a fresh batch of crunchy candy-coated popcorn with toasted nuts made at home is more satisfying than any supermarket variety. Serve it in bags with a little treat tucked in to keep your guests' eyes on the prize—I like to place little flea market charms and trinkets inside as a surprise.

> 10 cups freshly popped popcorn (from ⅓ cup unpopped kernels)
> ½ cup (1 stick) unsalted butter, cut into cubes
> 1 cup light brown sugar
> ½ cup light corn syrup
> ¼ cup molasses
> 1 teaspoon flaky sea salt (I like Maldon or fleur de sel), plus more
>   for finishing
> 1 teaspoon vanilla extract
> 1 cup toasted almonds

Note: To make stovetop popcorn, refer to the Sweet and Salty Kettle Corn recipe on page 90.

Preheat the oven to 350°F. Line 2 baking sheets with parchment paper.

Place the popcorn in a large heatproof bowl and set aside.

In a medium saucepan, melt the butter over medium heat. Stir in the brown sugar, corn syrup, molasses, and salt. Bring to a boil and continue to boil for 5 minutes. Remove from the heat and stir in the vanilla and almonds with a wooden spoon. Pour the caramel mixture over the popcorn and mix to coat evenly.

Spread the popcorn out over the 2 prepared baking sheets and bake for 15 minutes, gently turning the popcorn every 5 minutes. Let cool, then gently break up the popcorn. Finish with a sprinkle of flaky sea salt. Serve immediately or package into individual bags with little surprises for your guests.

june . july . august

SUMMER

And so with the sunshine and the great bursts of leaves growing

on the trees, just as things grow in fast movies, I had that

familiar conviction that life was beginning

over again with the summer.

F. SCOTT FITZGERALD

PICNIC IN CENTRAL PARK

⤝⤞

Central Park is a magical place. In the summertime picnicking on the grass is a pleasure excursion and an ideal way to take advantage of the warmer weather. Basking lazily in the sunshine on big blankets, people watching, nibbling, and reading make for a relaxing break in the city.

From my favorite spot in the park, these are some of the things I might see on an average day: early in the morning, men in suits scuffle past in loafers made of Italian leather; around noon, a rollerblading crew takes over a section of the park and skates in circles while showing off new tricks; moms and nannies in Spandex wheel strollers with two and three toddlers tucked inside; hot dog vendors and Italian ice pushers compete on corners; the faint rhythm of a trumpet player sounds off in the distance playing a melody of Frank Sinatra or Sammy Davis Jr. There's no better stage to host a picnic.

When packing lunch for an outing, I try to plan on dishes that don't require too much fuss. Pasta salad is simple, elegant, and forgiving. Not only does it travel well, but the combination of vegetables and pasta will keep you energized throughout the day. Sandwiches are another wonderful addition to the menu that requires only a few components and some good packaging. Match your main dishes with a citrus-spiked beverage and a little something sweet for dessert and you have a menu that is delightful and easy. Stretch out wide on your picnic blanket and hide your nose in a book, drift in and out of naps, and throw a Frisbee with friends in between. Have everyone dig into the picnic basket for some homemade treats and allow yourself an afternoon to sit back and enjoy the show.

Strawberry Limeade

Serves 4 to 6

Nothing quenches my thirst quite like limeade—it's just sweet and tart enough to be refreshing on a warm summer day, and I love the way the pretty pink of this drink adds a pop of color to a picnic. The strawberry lime puree is also excellent frozen into ice pops or sorbet.

    2 cups sliced fresh strawberries
    ¾ cup sugar
    Juice of 5 limes
    4 cups cold water
    1 lime, sliced into rounds

In a blender or food processor, puree the strawberries with the sugar and lime juice. Pour the strawberry puree into a large pitcher, add the cold water, and stir until mixed well. Transfer to a large glass bottle for picnicking and toss in the lime rounds.

Summer Pasta Salad

Serves 4 to 6 as a side

Pasta salad is the way to go for a picnic—it gets better as it sits and tastes great at room temperature. Also a plus on a day outdoors: the starch will sustain you and your guests so you can linger longer. *Orecchiette*, which translates from the Italian to "little ears," is pasta the size of a thumbprint and shaped like a cupped hand, perfect for catching bits of flavor so that every bite of this pasta sings with lemon, garlic, and mint. The pasta can be assembled ahead of time, the dressing kept in a separate jar, the garnishes on the side, and everything tossed together at the picnic site before serving.

8 ounces orecchiette pasta or other small shell pasta

Salt

⅓ cup extra virgin olive oil, plus more for tossing the pasta

Finely grated zest and juice of 1 lemon

1 shallot, minced

1 garlic clove, minced

Freshly ground pepper

½ pint mixed baby heirlooms tomatoes, cut in half

1 head frisée, coarsely chopped

8 ounces cooked or canned cannellini beans, rinsed and drained

2 tablespoons hazelnuts, toasted and chopped

2 tablespoons torn mint leaves

Shaved Parmesan cheese for garnish

Cook the pasta in a pot of boiling salted water until tender but firm to the bite, about 5 minutes. Drain, transfer to a large bowl, toss with a splash of olive oil to coat, then place in the freezer for a couple of minutes to cool.

Make the vinaigrette by whisking the olive oil with the lemon zest and juice, the shallot, and garlic. Season with salt and pepper. Add the tomatoes, frisée, and beans to the pasta and dress lightly with the vinaigrette. Garnish with the hazelnuts, mint, and cheese.

Prosciutto Cotto, Cilantro, *and* Pickled Fennel Sliders

Serves 6

Prosciutto cotto is an Italian cooked ham, perfectly paired with sharp pickled vegetables and fragrant herbs. Cilantro adds a fresh edge to the dish and fennel lends a mellow hint of licorice. These sliders can be wrapped in bundles with wax paper and tied with baker's twine to take on any outing.

1 fennel bulb, trimmed

½ cup rice vinegar

1 tablespoon sugar

Pinch of salt

½ cup mayonnaise

1 tablespoon fresh lime juice

1 teaspoon finely grated lime zest

Salt and freshly ground black pepper

12 mini brioche buns

8 ounces prosciutto cotto (or other cooked, sliced ham), thinly sliced

½ cup fresh cilantro sprigs

2 jalapeños, thinly sliced

Using a mandoline, thinly shave the fennel. In a medium bowl, whisk together the vinegar, sugar, and salt and toss with the fennel. Set aside for 15 minutes.

In a separate bowl, whisk together the mayonnaise, lime juice, and zest. Season with salt and pepper.

Assemble the sandwiches by spreading the bottom slices of brioche with lime mayonnaise, followed by some prosciutto slices and pickled fennel. Finish with cilantro and jalapeño slices and top with the brioche tops.

Tropical Trifles

Serves 6

What makes this dessert special is the packaging, though it's certainly delicious too. Trifles are beautiful on their own, but when layered into jars, they are not only adorable, they're travel ready. The mellow coconut cream in this recipe is brightened with passion fruit, a dreamily tropical combination.

SPECIAL EQUIPMENT: *Six 4½ -ounce jars*

One 15-ounce can full-fat coconut milk, refrigerated overnight

2 tablespoons sugar

1 teaspoon vanilla extract

1 cup raspberries

⅓ cup passion fruit or guava jam

1 cup crumbled shortbread cookies

Open the can of chilled coconut milk and scoop the solidified coconut cream that has risen to the top into a medium size bowl. Reserve any leftover coconut water for another use. Beat the coconut cream with an electric mixer on medium-high speed until soft peaks form, 3 to 4 minutes. Add the sugar and vanilla and mix until incorporated.

In a small bowl, mash the raspberries with the jam.

Line up your jars and layering ingredients among them. Layer each jar with crumbled shortbread, raspberry-jam mixture, and coconut cream, repeating the layering until the jars are filled. Close the jars with their lids and refrigerate until you are ready to leave for your picnic.

ROOFTOP BARBECUE

✎

*F*rom movies to drinking cocktails, gardening, and beekeeping, you name it and New Yorkers will find a rooftop to do it on. Of all the brilliant rooftop ideas, nothing trumps a barbecue overlooking the city. Everyone arrives in the late afternoon; the grill fires up and sends wafts of hot charcoal down to the street below. Friends dress the table with dishes brought from home. Fold-out chairs, stools, crates, and boxes serve as seating and everyone settles comfortably into the scene. When the haze of the sun begins to meet the horizon in an orange glow, the fixings on the grill make their way to the table and it's time to eat. There are never enough napkins to go around, and that's OK at a rooftop barbecue. Seconds and even thirds aren't uncouth. There's plenty of food, and when the playlist reaches its final songs, everyone is satiated and happy.

When it comes to the menu for a barbecue feast, I love playing with a mix of the bright flavors of summer and the deep, complex flavors from the grill. In a grilled watermelon salad, the juices in the melon break down and caramelize, becoming deep and near savory. Grilled seafood and meat are livened up with salsas and slaws. And nothing says barbecue quite like ribs, with a sauce that will travel from the plate to your chin, cheeks, fingers, and arms—the stickiness blends with the heat of the summer night. Dessert is light, herbaceous, and just sweet enough to close the feast.

The barbecues I've had the pleasure to enjoy over the years—from the beaches of California to the rooftops of New York—are the inspiration behind this menu. These recipes are perfect for a crowd and more than ideal for a rooftop or any other barbecue venue—just be sure to keep the cold beer coming and the music blasting.

Grilled Fennel *and* Watermelon Salad

Serves 6

When the heat settles in, all I want to eat is watermelon—it's fresh, thirst quenching, and incredibly adaptable, as highlighted in this hidden gem of a recipe. Grilled watermelon, with its sweet caramelized exterior, plays off the spice of the jalapeño, the zest of the citrus, the saltiness of the olives, and the creaminess of the cheese, making this salad burst with flavor in every bite.

2 medium fennel bulbs, trimmed and sliced vertically into
    ½-inch pieces

½ medium seedless watermelon (about 2½ pounds), cut into
    ½-inch wedges, rind removed

⅓ cup extra virgin olive oil, plus more for brushing

Salt and freshly ground black pepper

2 tablespoons honey

¼ cup fresh lime juice

1 tablespoon finely chopped jalapeño

8 ounces watercress, tough stems trimmed

½ cup crumbled feta cheese

¼ cup pitted kalamata olives

1 tablespoon chopped fresh mint leaves

Prepare a medium fire in a charcoal grill, or heat a gas grill to medium. Brush the fennel and watermelon with olive oil and season with salt and pepper. Grill the fennel for 2 to 3 minutes on each side, until lightly charred, then grill the watermelon until lightly charred, about 2 minutes on each side. Set aside with the fennel.

To make the dressing, in a small bowl, whisk the olive oil with the honey, lime juice, and jalapeño. Season with salt and pepper.

To serve, place the watercress on a platter and top with the grilled fennel and watermelon. Drizzle the dressing over the salad and top with cheese, olives, and mint.

Whole Fish *with* Lemon Salsa

Serves 6

When it comes to the grill, a whole fish is greater than its parts and is fun to share at a communal table. In this recipe, herbs and lemon are tucked into and wrapped around the fish, acting as a guard to the flesh and allowing for a fragrant, tender meat. The bright lemon salsa brings out the fresh flavors of any seafood and can even be enjoyed with chips.

Three 2½- to 3-pound whole mackerels, cleaned and gutted

Extra virgin olive oil for brushing

Kosher salt and freshly ground black pepper

1 bunch fresh thyme

1 bunch fresh oregano

3 lemons, sliced into thin rounds

Lemon Salsa (recipe follows)

SPECIAL EQUIPMENT: *Kitchen twine*

Rinse the fish under cold running water and pat dry with paper towels. Brush the fish with olive oil and season with salt and pepper inside and out. Place 3 to 4 sprigs of thyme and oregano and 2 lemon rounds into each fish cavity. Layer the remaining herbs and lemon rounds around the outside of fish and secure with kitchen string. This will help protect the fish from overcooking on the grill and give it extra flavor.

Prepare a medium fire in a charcoal grill, or heat a gas grill to medium. Grill the fish on an oiled rack until just cooked through, 5 to 7 minutes on each side. Cut and discard the string and lay the fish on a platter. Serve with Lemon Salsa.

LEMON SALSA (*Makes 1 cup*)

¹/₃ cup chopped red onion

2 tablespoons chopped fresh parsley

1 tablespoon chopped fresh cilantro

1 tablespoon finely chopped jalapeño

¹/₃ cup extra virgin olive oil

4 lemons, peeled, pith removed, and segmented

Salt and freshly ground black pepper

In a small bowl, combine all the ingredients. Let sit for at least 10 minutes for the flavors to combine before serving. It can be made up to 2 days ahead of time and storied in an airtight container in the refrigerator.

BBQ Ribs *with* Coffee Mole Sauce *and* Jicama Slaw

Serves 6

Ribs are a barbecue staple for a simple reason: they are delicious. On top of this, I tend to think ribs are a great BBQ offering because they're an excuse to get messy and give in to your primal urges while eating with your hands—perfect in an outdoor setting. Here the richness of the cocoa and bitterness of the coffee combine to create a smoky, decadent sauce for coating your ribs. The jicama slaw that accompanies the ribs serves as a crunchy and refreshing palette cleanser.

> 2 tablespoons extra virgin olive oil
>
> 1 small onion, diced
>
> 2 garlic cloves, minced
>
> 2 tablespoons cocoa powder
>
> ¾ cup brewed espresso or strong dark coffee
>
> ¾ cup ketchup
>
> 2 tablespoons apple cider vinegar
>
> 2 tablespoons Worcestershire sauce
>
> 2 tablespoons brown sugar
>
> 3 dried ancho chiles, chopped
>
> 1½ teaspoons mustard powder
>
> ½ teaspoon ground cinnamon
>
> Salt and freshly ground black pepper
>
> 4 pounds baby back pork ribs

Heat the olive oil in a medium saucepan over medium heat. Add the onion and garlic and sauté until softened, 2 to 3 minutes. Reduce the heat to medium-low, add the cocoa powder and coffee, and cook for about 5 minutes to release the cocoa flavor, stirring occasionally. Stir in the ketchup, vinegar, Worcestershire sauce, brown sugar, chiles, mustard powder, and cinnamon. Reduce the heat to low, cover, and simmer for 5 minutes. Remove from the heat and season with salt and pepper. Cool, then pour ¾ cup of the sauce into a container, cover, and refrigerate for later use. Brush the ribs generously with the remaining sauce, cover, and refrigerate overnight.

Preheat the oven to 350°F.

Wrap the ribs in foil, place them on a baking sheet, and bake for 1 hour. Lower the oven temperature to 300°F and continue to bake for another hour. Remove the ribs from the foil and drain the drippings.

Prepare a medium fire in a charcoal grill, or heat a gas grill to medium. Set aside a portion of the reserved sauce to brush onto both sides of the ribs. Place the ribs on an oiled rack and cook for 5 to 7 minutes on each side, brushing with the reserved sauce, until grill marks appear. Serve the ribs with the remaining reserved sauce and some Jicama Slaw (recipe follows).

JICAMA SLAW

2 tablespoons fresh lime juice

¼ cup rice vinegar

1 tablespoon sugar

2 tablespoons extra virgin olive oil

Salt and freshly ground black pepper

3 cups julienned jicama

½ cup thinly sliced red onion

1 cup julienned carrot

2 tablespoons chopped fresh cilantro

In a small bowl, whisk together the lime juice, vinegar, sugar, and olive oil; season with salt and pepper. In a large bowl, combine the jicama, red onion, and carrot. Toss with the dressing and let sit for 5 minutes for the flavors to combine. Finish by topping with the cilantro

Cantaloupe Campari Granita *with* Basil Cream

Serves 6

I like serving granita as a lighter alternative to ice cream on sweltering summer days—the flaked ice crystals are deliciously refreshing. It's also effortless and requires no special equipment to make it. The mellow melon flavor is paired with Campari, a bittersweet Italian aperitif, and finished with a cool dollop of basil cream. Make an extra batch with any of your favorite sweet summer fruits and keep in the freezer to enjoy anytime.

1 ¼ cups sugar

2 tablespoons fresh lemon juice

1 cup water

1 cantaloupe (about 3 pounds)

¼ cup Campari

Basil Cream (recipe follows)

Small fresh basil leaves for garnish

In a small saucepan, stir together the sugar, lemon juice, and water; bring to a boil over medium-high heat and continue to stir until the sugar has dissolved. Remove from the heat and let the syrup cool.

Meanwhile, cut the melon into rough cubes, discarding the seeds and rind. Place in the bowl of a food processor or blender and process until smooth. In a large bowl, mix together the sugar syrup, melon puree, and Campari. Pour into a shallow container, cover, and place in the freezer. Stir and rake the flaky crystals with a fork every 30 minutes to lighten the texture, for up to 2 hours, until the mixture is frozen. Scrape the finished granita into bowls, top with a dollop of basil cream, and garnish with basil leaves. The granita can be made ahead of time and stored in the freezer; rake with fork again before serving.

BASIL CREAM

1 cup heavy cream

2 tablespoons sugar

¼ cup fresh basil leaves

In a small saucepan, combine the cream and sugar and bring to a simmer over medium heat, stirring until the sugar dissolves. Bruise the basil leaves with the back of a wooden spoon and stir them into the cream mixture. Remove from the heat and let steep for 20 minutes. Remove the basil leaves and set aside to cool. Transfer the cream to a container and chill in the refrigerator until cold, about 6 hours or overnight.

Before serving, whisk the Basil Cream with an electric mixer on high speed until soft peaks form.

Our Grilling Favorites

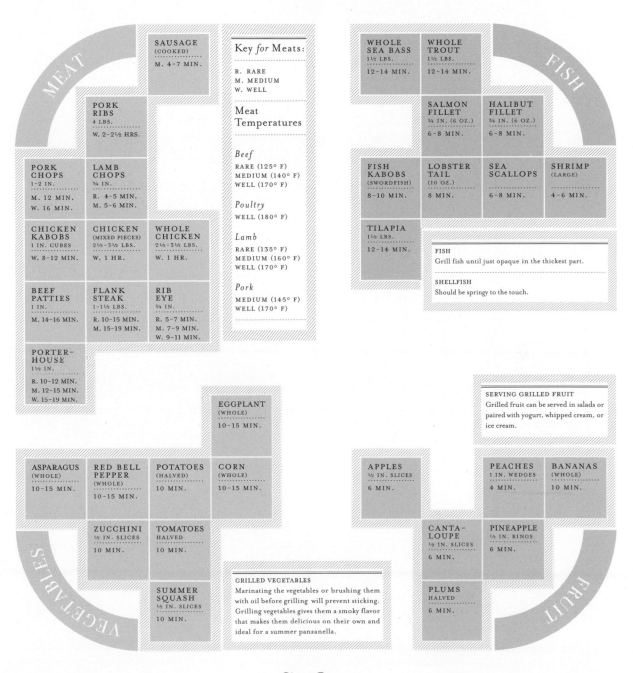

MEAT

SAUSAGE
(COOKED)
M. 4–7 MIN.

PORK RIBS
4 LBS.
W. 2–2½ HRS.

PORK CHOPS
1–2 IN.
M. 12 MIN.
W. 16 MIN.

LAMB CHOPS
¾ IN.
R. 4–5 MIN.
M. 5–6 MIN.

CHICKEN KABOBS
1 IN. CUBES
W. 8–12 MIN.

CHICKEN
(MIXED PIECES)
2½–3½ LBS.
W. 1 HR.

WHOLE CHICKEN
2½–3½ LBS.
W. 1 HR.

BEEF PATTIES
1 IN.
M. 14–16 MIN.

FLANK STEAK
1–1½ LBS.
R. 10–15 MIN.
M. 15–19 MIN.

RIB EYE
¾ IN.
R. 5–7 MIN.
M. 7–9 MIN.
W. 9–11 MIN.

PORTER-HOUSE
1½ IN.
R. 10–12 MIN.
M. 12–15 MIN.
W. 15–19 MIN.

Key for Meats:

R. RARE
M. MEDIUM
W. WELL

Meat Temperatures

Beef
RARE (125° F)
MEDIUM (140° F)
WELL (170° F)

Poultry
WELL (180° F)

Lamb
RARE (135° F)
MEDIUM (160° F)
WELL (170° F)

Pork
MEDIUM (145° F)
WELL (170° F)

FISH

WHOLE SEA BASS
1½ LBS.
12–14 MIN.

WHOLE TROUT
1½ LBS.
12–14 MIN.

SALMON FILLET
¾ IN. (6 OZ.)
6–8 MIN.

HALIBUT FILLET
¾ IN. (6 OZ.)
6–8 MIN.

FISH KABOBS
(SWORDFISH)
8–10 MIN.

LOBSTER TAIL
(10 OZ.)
8 MIN.

SEA SCALLOPS
6–8 MIN.

SHRIMP
(LARGE)
4–6 MIN.

TILAPIA
1½ LBS.
12–14 MIN.

FISH
Grill fish until just opaque in the thickest part.

SHELLFISH
Should be springy to the touch.

VEGETABLES

EGGPLANT
(WHOLE)
10–15 MIN.

ASPARAGUS
(WHOLE)
10–15 MIN.

RED BELL PEPPER
(WHOLE)
10–15 MIN.

POTATOES
(HALVED)
10 MIN.

CORN
(WHOLE)
10–15 MIN.

ZUCCHINI
½ IN. SLICES
10 MIN.

TOMATOES
HALVED
10 MIN.

SUMMER SQUASH
½ IN. SLICES
10 MIN.

GRILLED VEGETABLES
Marinating the vegetables or brushing them with oil before grilling will prevent sticking. Grilling vegetables gives them a smoky flavor that makes them delicious on their own and ideal for a summer panzanella.

SERVING GRILLED FRUIT
Grilled fruit can be served in salads or paired with yogurt, whipped cream, or ice cream.

APPLES
½ IN. SLICES
6 MIN.

PEACHES
1 IN. WEDGES
4 MIN.

BANANAS
(WHOLE)
10 MIN.

CANTA-LOUPE
½ IN. SLICES
6 MIN.

PINEAPPLE
½ IN. RINGS
6 MIN.

PLUMS
HALVED
6 MIN.

FRUIT

Chart No. 004

BEACH DAY

※

When my friends and I have a beach day, we plan to spend six or seven hours on the sand. We lounge. We go surfing. We play in the waves. We lay like starfish on our towels. The day passes until our shadows disappear on the surf.

The snacks I packed earlier in the morning turn into a mess of sand throughout the day. We nibble a little here and there on strawberries and chips and frozen grapes, but by the time we've folded up our towels and put our beach chairs in the trunk of the car, we are ravenous.

The post-beach meal is a refueling, a necessity. After a day in the sun, I crave flavors that are lively and laced with citrus and spice. Foods that are cool, even chilled, are ideal. Ceviche is a dish that comes off as intimidating but is simple and incredibly refreshing. In the summer tomatillos are easy to find at the farmers' market or at a roadside stand. Their sourness is a lovely surprise in salsa, one of my favorite seaside staples.

The following recipes are inspired by long days in the sand and surf. They are everything I crave with a bit of sunburn. Enjoy this food with close friends on the beach, a patio, or in the kitchen with the windows open, hair still salt-licked and sand trapped beneath your fingernails.

E GREAT GATSBY

otion. But in the new si
in the house too.
naking every possible n
g over the stove—but I don
ey were sitting at either end o
other as if some question had been
nd every vestige of embarrassment
s smeared with tears, and when I
I began wiping at it with her hand-
there was a change in Gatsby that
He literally glowed; without a
n a new well-being radiated from
.

aid, as if he hadn't seen me for
he was going to shake hands.

what I was talking about

Tomatillo Salsa

Serves 4 to 6

Tomatillos take a backseat to their red counterparts, tomatoes, most of the time. No longer. Wrapped up in a paper-like skin, tomatillos are crisp and sour, and they are perfect for making salsa. Nibble on this salsa with tortilla chips while you're prepping the rest of your post-beach meal, or make it in the morning and bring it to the beach for a snack between catching waves and building sand castles.

1½ pounds tomatillos, husked and rinsed

2 fresh serrano chiles, stemmed, seeded, and cut in half

2 garlic cloves, roughly chopped

½ small onion, finely chopped

½ cup finely chopped fresh cilantro

2 tablespoons fresh lime juice

Salt and freshly ground black pepper

Preheat the broiler.

Arrange the tomatillos and chiles on a baking sheet, place under the broiler, and broil for 3 to 4 minutes on each side, until slightly blackened. Transfer to a food processor along with the garlic and onion and pulse until well blended but still chunky. Add the cilantro and lime juice and pulse once or twice to mix them in. Season with salt and pepper. Serve with corn tortilla chips.

Mixed Seafood Ceviche

Serves 4 to 6

Ceviche is coastal soul food. Where seafood is abundant, ceviche should be too—it's the perfect preparation for fresh-from-the-ocean catch, because it's "cooked" with just the acid from the citrus. I've chosen to mix several types of seafood in this ceviche, but feel free to stick to a single type or a mixture of your favorites or what's locally available.

4 ounces squid, cleaned and cut into rings

4 ounces sea scallops

4 ounces shrimp, peeled and deveined

8 ounces red snapper

1 cup fresh lime juice

½ cup fresh lemon juice

1 serrano chile, stemmed, seeded, and finely diced

1 garlic clove, finely minced

2 tablespoons finely chopped red bell pepper

½ cup finely chopped red onion

1 tablespoon salt, plus more if needed

Freshly ground black pepper

Extra virgin olive oil for drizzling

¼ cup chopped fresh cilantro

In a large bowl, toss the seafood with the lime and lemon juices, cover, and refrigerate for 2 to 3 hours, until the meat has become opaque.

Add the chile, garlic, bell pepper, onion, and salt and toss well; refrigerate for another 30 minutes. Season with pepper, taste, and adjust the seasonings as needed. Finish with a drizzle of olive oil, top with the cilantro, and serve.

How to Prepare

SHRIMP

TO PREPARE FRESH SHRIMP, first peel off the outer shell and pull the tail off with your hands. Devein the shrimp by slicing halfway through the shrimp from mid-head to tail, revealing a small black vein, and pulling out and discarding the vein.

Blackened Fish Tacos

Serves 4 to 6

Growing up in California, I lived off fish tacos for entire summers—they are *the* classic California food. After playing in the ocean all afternoon, I'd find my favorite taco stand serving the freshest Mexican food and devour fish tacos. This recipe is a throwback to those afternoons on the West Coast, combining the smoke of the blackened fish with the sweet, piquant flavors of pineapple salsa and radishes.

> 1 fresh pineapple, peeled, quartered lengthwise, and cored
>
> 1 jalapeño, seeded and finely diced
>
> ½ red onion, finely diced
>
> Finely grated zest and juice of 2 limes, plus extra lime wedges for serving
>
> Salt and freshly ground black pepper
>
> 1½ pounds tilapia fillets or other white flaky fish
>
> Extra virgin olive oil for brushing
>
> 2 tablespoons Cajun seasoning (I like Tony Chachere's Creole Seasoning)
>
> 12 corn tortillas
>
> 1 bunch radish, trimmed and thinly sliced
>
> ½ cup fresh cilantro leaves

Prepare a medium-hot fire in a charcoal grill, or heat a gas grill to medium-high heat and brush the grates with oil. Alternatively, preheat an oiled grill pan on a stovetop over medium-high heat. Place the pineapple quarters on the grill and cook until lightly charred on all sides, 2 to 4 minutes per side. Cool to room temperature, then cut the pineapple into medium dice. In a large bowl, toss the pineapple with the jalapeño, onion, lime juice, and zest and season with salt and pepper. Cover and refrigerate until ready to use.

Heat a charcoal or gas grill to medium-high heat again and brush with oil.

Rinse the fish and pat it dry. Brush with olive oil and rub with Cajun seasoning, salt, and pepper. Grill the fish for about 4 minutes on one side, until blackened, then flip and grill to blacken the other side, about 2 minutes. Transfer to a plate and let rest for 5 minutes, then flake the fish with a fork. Place the tortillas on the grill and heat quickly, about 20 seconds.

Divide the fish among the tortillas and top with the grilled pineapple salsa, radish slices, and cilantro; serve with the lime wedges.

Cocktail Ice Pops

Rather than shaking up a cocktail, serve it on a stick. Experiment with your favorite cocktail recipes and keep these beauties stocked in your freezer to quench your thirst on the hottest days. Here are a couple of my favorite summertime mixes.

SPECIAL EQUIPMENT: *6 ice pop molds and 6 wooden sticks*

BLACKBERRY BRAMBLE ICE POPS (*Makes 6 ice pops*)

¾ cup fresh lemon juice

1 cup water

¾ cup superfine sugar

¼ cup gin

1½ cups fresh blackberries

In a pitcher, mix together the lemon juice, water, sugar, and gin, stirring to dissolve the sugar. Pour the mixture into the ice pop molds, leaving 2 inches for the blackberries. Freeze until partially frozen, about 1 hour. Meanwhile, mash the blackberries with a fork until broken down and chunky. Top off the ice pops with the mashed blackberries and insert the wooden sticks. Return the ice pops to the freezer and freeze for at least 3 hours, until frozen through.

SPECIAL EQUIPMENT: *6 ice pop molds and 6 wooden sticks*

MARGARITA ICE POPS (*Makes 6 ice pops*)

¾ cup fresh lime juice

1 cup water

¾ cup superfine sugar

3 tablespoons tequila

1 tablespoon Cointreau

Thinly sliced lime rounds

Coarse salt for serving

In a pitcher, mix together the lime juice, water, sugar, tequila, and Cointreau, stirring to dissolve the sugar. Pour the mixture into the molds, leaving 1 inch for the lime rounds. Freeze until partially frozen, about 1 hour. Using a butter knife, press the lime rounds into each mold against the sides. Top off the ice pops with some more of the margarita mixture and insert the wooden sticks. Return the ice pops to the freezer and freeze for at least 3 hours, until frozen through. Serve sprinkled with coarse salt.

FARMERS' MARKET FEAST

⇝

*S*ummer is peak season at the farmers' market. Strawberries are at their sweetest. Tomatoes burst through their skin with juice. Squash appears in a multitude of shapes, sizes, and colors. Melons become fragrant and soft around the navel. Long and lean green and yellow beans overflow baskets. And stone fruits, still attached to their leaves, are piled into barrels, ripe for the picking.

The scene at the market in late summer is dangerous territory for me. The onslaught of perfect produce lures me in, and before I know it I have three bags dangling from each arm, filled with items I hadn't planned on buying. When this happens, I inevitably invite friends over and set out to make a farmers' market feast to share my bounty.

Those items I hadn't thought I really needed but could not resist turn into necessities: tomatoes transform into a salad, sliced into thick wedges and drizzled with good olive oil and a sprinkling of sea salt; zucchini and other summer squash become a simple but substantial dish when paired with a protein-rich grain like quinoa; and for dessert, squash blossoms, fried and served with ricotta and honey toe the line between sweet and savory. We uncork a couple bottles of crisp white wine and shuffle dishes around like a family.

Farmers' market feasts are effortless to prepare—the freshness of the ingredients means they need little meddling to shine and taste their best. The hardest part of it is not eating all of the produce before your guests arrive.

Heirloom Tomato *and* Burrata Salad

Serves 6

When heirloom tomatoes are in season, they need nothing but a sprinkle of salt to be enjoyed; hence this classic combination: tomatoes + mozzarella + basil. In this recipe I've used burrata cheese, which has an outer shell of solid mozzarella and an oozy creamy interior made of a combination of mozzarella and cream. It melts in your mouth and complements the tangy sweetness of the tomatoes. Simple ingredients at their best are all that's needed for a dish to inspire. Prepare this recipe with whatever tomato varieties grace your market or your garden this season.

  4 large mixed heirloom tomatoes
  8 ounces burrata mozzarella or other fresh mozzarella, sliced
  High-quality extra virgin olive oil for drizzling
  Flaky salt, preferably Maldon
  Freshly ground black pepper
  ½ cup fresh basil leaves, roughly torn

Core the tomatoes and cut them into wedges. Arrange the tomatoes on a platter layered with slices of burrata and drizzle with olive oil. Let stand at room temperature for 20 minutes. Finish with some salt and pepper and top with the basil.

Shaved Summer Squash *with* Quinoa *and* Feta

Serves 6

Unlike hardy winter squash, summer squash is harvested while the exterior is still tender, and can be eaten rind, seeds, and all. The first time I saw the multitude of varieties of these colorful squash, I excitedly bought as many as I could, from bright yellow crookneck squash and green zucchini to the petite and nutty pattypan squash. I've found the round-shaped squash are delicious when hollowed out, stuffed, and baked, and the long yellow squash and zucchini make a wonderfully light side dish when shaved raw into ribbons and tossed with dressing.

½ cup dry quinoa

Salt

2 tablespoons fresh lemon juice

I garlic clove, minced

¼ cup extra virgin olive oil

Freshly ground black pepper

2 tablespoons pine nuts

1½ pounds mixed summer squash

¼ cup (I ounce) crumbled feta cheese

¼ cup roughly chopped fresh mint

Rinse the quinoa thoroughly. Put it in a small saucepan with I cup of water and a pinch of salt and bring to a boil over medium-high heat. Cover the pan, turn the heat down to low, and simmer for 15 minutes. Remove from heat, cover, and let sit for 5 minutes, then fluff with a fork.

Meanwhile, in a small bowl, whisk together the lemon juice, garlic, and olive oil. Season with salt and pepper and set aside.

In a small skillet, toast the pine nuts over medium-high heat, shaking the pan frequently, for about 2 minutes, until lightly browned. Remove from the heat and set aside.

With a vegetable peeler, shave the squash lengthwise into long strips. In a large bowl, toss the shaved squash with the dressing and let stand for a few minutes. Add the quinoa and toss. Finish by scattering the pine nuts, feta cheese, and mint on top.

Grilled Chicken *with* Preserved Lemon

Serves 6

Grilled chicken is a simple dish every cook should master. The ideal chicken should have tender and juicy meat with a nice charred exterior. They key to great chicken is to marinate it before grilling, as it adds a depth of flavor and helps to seal in the moisture while cooking. I like to let it marinate overnight before cooking to let the flavors deepen. Preserved lemons are one of the indispensable ingredients of Moroccan cooking, and their distinctive pickled taste brings bright summer flavors to this classic grilled chicken dish. It's a twist on a classic summertime staple.

5 small preserved lemons (either homemade; see below, or
    purchased at a Middle Eastern market)
3 garlic cloves, peeled
Salt
Juice of 3 lemons
2 tablespoons honey
2 teaspoons cumin seeds, toasted and ground
2 teaspoons paprika
¼ cup extra virgin olive oil
2 whole chickens (about 3 pounds each), cut into 8 pieces each
Freshly ground black pepper
½ cup roughly chopped fresh cilantro

Rinse the preserved lemons well under cold running water. Discard the pulp from inside the lemons and give the rinds a rough chop. Using a mortar and pestle or the side of a knife, mash the garlic cloves with a generous pinch of salt to a paste. Transfer the preserved lemons and garlic paste to a food processor, add the lemon juice, honey, cumin, paprika, and olive oil, and process until smooth.

Rub the lemon marinade all over the chicken pieces and season with salt and pepper. Transfer the chicken to a dish, cover, and leave it to marinate in the refrigerator for about 6 hours, or overnight if you prefer.

Prepare a medium-hot fire in a charcoal grill, or preheat a grill pan (in which case you will have to cook the chickens one at a time) over medium-high heat. Remove the chicken from the marinade and grill until just cooked through, 5 to 8 minutes per side. Turn the heat to medium-low and continue to cook the chicken until it's cooked through and the juices run clear when a fork is inserted into the meat, about 25 minutes more. Transfer the chicken to a serving platter and finish with the cilantro.

How to Make

PRESERVED LEMONS

TO MAKE YOUR OWN PRESERVED LEMONS, use about 6 lemons for a quart-size jar. First soak the lemons in water for 2 days to soften the peel (if using Meyer lemons, you can skip this step). Quarter the lemons from the top, leaving them intact by cutting to within ½ inch from the bottom. Generously rub kosher salt, about 2 tablespoons for each lemon, onto the exposed flesh. Add other spices, such as a cinnamon stick, cloves, coriander, peppercorns, and bay leaves to the jar if you like. Cover the lemons with enough fresh lemon juice to submerge the lemons. Let the lemons sit on the countertop, shaking the jar occasionally, for 30 days. To use the lemons, give a rinse under running water and remove and discard the pulp. Preserved lemons will keep refrigerated for up to 1 year.

Fried Squash Blossoms *with* Ricotta *and* Honey

Serves 6

Squash blossoms signal of the arrival of summer. The bright orange blossoms come from summer squash plants like zucchini and are typically served as a stuffed and fried savory appetizer. In our version, we've made it into a dessert, with its delicate battered and fried petals sitting on a dollop of sweetened ricotta.

SPECIAL EQUIPMENT: *Deep-fry or candy thermometer*

FOR THE RICOTTA

1½ cups fresh ricotta cheese

3 tablespoons sugar

Finely grated zest and juice of 1 small orange

Finely grated zest of 1 lemon

FOR THE SQUASH BLOSSOMS

½ cup all-purpose flour

2 tablespoons confectioners' sugar, plus more for dusting

Pinch of salt

⅓ cup club soda

6 squash blossoms

Vegetable oil for frying

Honey for drizzling

In a medium bowl, stir together the ricotta, sugar, orange zest and juice, and lemon zest. Set aside until ready to use.

In a separate medium bowl, whisk together the flour, confectioners' sugar, and salt. Whisk in the club soda until just combined. The batter should be runny but thick enough to coat the squash blossoms.

In a large pot, heat about 2 inches oil over medium-high heat until it begins to shimmer and a deep-fry thermometer reads 375°F. Working in small batches, dip the squash blossoms into the flour batter to coat, then shake off any excess batter. Without crowding the pan, fry the blossoms until golden and crisp, 1 to 2 minutes. Remove with a slotted spoon and transfer to a paper towel–lined plate to drain. Repeat with the remaining squash blossoms.

Place a generous dollop of ricotta cream on each plate. Top with the crisp squash blossoms, dust with confectioners' sugar, and drizzle with honey. Serve immediately.

ACKNOWLEDGMENTS

A very special thanks to:

Sara Bercholz, my amazing editor and publisher, for believing in my work from the very start and patiently guiding me through the making of this book. Your kindness, patience, and uplifting spirit has made working on this book a pleasure.

Abigail Koons, my literary agent, for sharing your wisdom and working with me through the whole book-making process.

Mom and Dad, for raising us with such dedication, love, and support. I'm lucky to have grown up in such a sunny and laughter-filled household. A very special thanks to my Hong Kong family: the Chan, Siu, and Law families, for their support in my creative pursuits and nurturing me from afar.

The twins, Debbie and Donna Yen, my lovely sisters. I appreciate all the years of behind the scenes work. For washing piles of dishes, crafting until 2 A.M., and sorting through my spreadsheets. I am lucky to have always had you by my sides.

Lisel Arroyo, thank you for helping me to build The Jewels of New York from the very start. A true friend and partner, I am so proud of all that we've accomplished together. I look forward to collaborating and making magic together until we are old and gray. Cheers to the world we created from our imaginations.

Quy Nguyen, you are one of the most influential and generous people I've had the pleasure to know. I am so grateful for the beautiful world you've shared with me through your eyes. You give a new life to the long forgotten. My mentor and best friend, thank you for inspiring me to always dream.

Jade Lai and Creatures of Comfort, you encouraged me to go bold and take risks, and I've finally found my voice through it all. Thank you for being supportive and gracefully tolerating me cooking next to all the fancy clothes. Your impeccable style and taste influence all that cross your path.

JONY Crew: Hannah Schmitz and Kali Solack, for testing and tackling through all the recipes in this book. Justin Hicks, for your detailed eye and delicious food. Ashley Schleeper, for helping me to shape the words in this book. You all made it happen.

Thanks to the people who contributed beautiful photographs to this book. Liz Adler and Christopher Testani, thank you for sharing your talents through styling and photography in our Harvest Celebration story. Tom Hines and Michelle Lueking, for making us look good.

Thank you for your generous contributions in making this beautiful book. Sarah Ryhanen at Saipua. Your flowers make me acknowledge all the precious beauty in the world. Andre Burgos, I appreciate your dedication to collecting all the little things that give our meals enjoyment. Confetti System, Julie Ho and Nicholas Andersen, thank you for the beautiful decorations that make every party sparkle. Nanse Kawashima, your gifted eye and bright ideas added life to the Beach and Cookie stories. To the Foundry LIC, for lending us your space to shoot in.

All of my East Coast friends have given me so much support, positive energy, and endless inspiration. I am grateful to have met all of you through my years here. Thanks to my New York family: Anh Tuan Pham, Eri Nagasaka, Ninh and Erik Wysocan, Andrea Huelse, Claudia Wu, Katherine Wakid, Scott Newlin, Emily Anderson, Byron and Lissette Parr, Daniel Haggerty, the Serrano-McClain family, Lars Beaulieu, Sylvia Rooney, Adrian Gaut, Tristan Schmitz, Andrew Stewart, and Danny Bowien.

My West Coast peeps, you live on the other side but are just as important: Ethan Ayer, Catherine Hahn, Adam Reineck, Thomas Stern, Nathan Gray, Laura Steiner, Portia Wells, Joseph Pitruzzelli, and Nathan Williams at *Kinfolk Magazine.*

To my wonderful clients and all those who have been faithfully following my work at The Jewels of New York since its beginning.

RECIPES BY CATEGORY

⨯

BEVERAGES

INDEX OF TIPS

INDEX

Walnut Oatmeal Cookies, Fig, 80–81

Watermelon Salad, and Grilled Fennel, 219–221

Whole Fish with Lemon Salsa, 222–23

Wild Mushroom Risotto with Caramelized Leeks, 105–7

Wild Rice Stuffing, 63–65

winter

celebrations during, 114

mealtimes during, 85

Yen, Diana, vision, 11

Yogurt, Turkish-Style Eggs with, 165–66